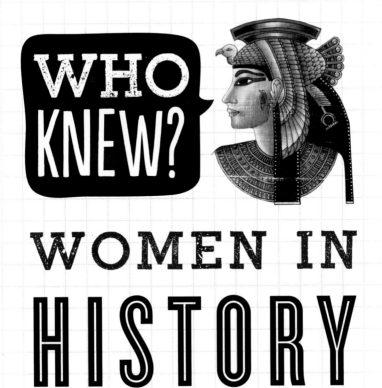

WHO KNEW?

WOMEN IN HISTORY

Sarah Herman

PORTABLE
PRESS

Portable Press
An imprint of Printers Row Publishing Group
A division of Readerlink Distribution Services, LLC
10350 Barnes Canyon Road, Suite 100, San Diego, CA 92121
www.portablepress.com

PORTABLE
PRESS

Correspondence concerning the content of this book or permissions should be
addressed to Portable Press, Editorial Department, at the above address. Author and
illustration inquiries should be addressed to The Bright Press, part of The Quarto
Group, Level 1, Ovest House, 58 West Street, Brighton, UK, BN1 2RA.

Publisher: Peter Norton
Associate Publisher: Ana Parker
Editor: JoAnn Padgett
Publishing Team: Vicki Jaeger, Lauren Taniguchi, Stephanie Romero

Conceived and designed by The Bright Press, part of The Quarto Group,
Level 1, Ovest House, 58 West Street, Brighton, UK, BN1 2RA
Publisher: Mark Searle
Creative Director: James Evans
Managing Editor: Jacqui Sayers
In-house Editor: Judith Chamberlain
Project Editor: Lucy York
Cover and Interior Design: Lindsey Johns and Clare Barber

Text: Sarah Herman

ISBN: 978-1-68412-787-0

Library of Congress Cataloging-in-Publication Data
Names: Herman, Sarah, 1984- author.
Title: Women in history / Sarah Herman.
Description: San Diego, CA : Portable Press, 2019. | Series: Who knew?
Identifiers: LCCN 2018056928 | ISBN 9781684127870 (paperback)
Subjects: LCSH: Women--Biography--Miscellanea. | Women--History--Miscellanea.
| BISAC: REFERENCE / Trivia. | REFERENCE / Curiosities & Wonders.
Classification: LCC CT3230 .H47 2019 | DDC 920.72 [B] --dc23 LC record available
at https://lccn.loc.gov/2018056928

Printed in China
First Printing: July 2019
23 22 21 20 19   1 2 3 4 5

"Be less curious about people and more curious about ideas.**"**

–Marie Curie

CONTENTS

INTRODUCTION

For centuries, men's chisels, quills, pens, and typewriters were used to write women out of history deliberately and by omission. This collection of female-focused facts, tales, and tidbits attempts to redress the balance. Stuffed with all things unusual, unbelievable, and unprecedented, this is the anecdotal almanac to keep you on your toes and regale you with one-off wonders, strange stories, and weird womanly happenings from the last two millennia.

From the first computer program to discovering the DNA double helix, and from the world's first novel to the one that started a war, women's achievements, inventions, and art have long been sidelined or overshadowed by the work of their male contemporaries. But not in this book. It celebrates female leadership on the battlefield, at the highest echelons of government, and in the streets of revolution. With questions about Queen Victoria, Catherine the Great, Joan of Arc, and Boudicca, it covers the gamut of power players. Whether it's ruling a country, founding a religion, or leading the charge against the Romans, the Nazis, or misogyny, there's a woman who's done it and done it well.

At times in history when opportunities for women were few, some refused to be pigeonholed. Women climbed to the top of Everest, traveled around the world in less than eighty days, and threw themselves over Niagara Falls in a barrel, just because they could (or because others thought they couldn't). And then there are the daring and dastardly—the cops, the murderesses, the pirates, and the privileged few

who abused their power. Find out about the real women of the Wild West, the Salem "witches," the Hungarian countess who bathed in the blood of her victims, and the private detective who foiled a presidential assassination attempt.

With chapters from Politics to Show Business, and everything in between, *Who Knew?: Women in History* is the definitive destination for those who want to get up close and personal with the ladies who've made, slayed, and sashayed their way into the history books. Each chapter is rounded off with a short quiz, so you can test yourself and your friends. Make sure you know your Marie Curie from your Marie Tharp, your Boudicca from your Borden, and your Rosie the Riveter from your Sadie the Goat. Then, turn to the back of the book for the answers.

Try as you might to be satisfied with the knowledge you already possess about some of history's most brilliant, brave, and brutal women, we've got an inkling you want to know more. And you're in the right place. The treasures contained herein are sure to shock, inspire, and delight, as well as boost your feminist credentials. So put aside thoughts of men in lab coats, men in uniform, men wielding paintbrushes, and men wearing crowns (well, men doing anything, really) and prepare to embark on a brain-opening odyssey into the world of women in history.

WHO WERE "THE BUTTERFLIES" AND WHY WERE THEY ASSASSINATED?

HOW DID A LOVE FOR CIDER LEAD TO THE FIRST WOMAN BEING ELECTED MAYOR IN THE UNITED STATES?

WHO WAS THE ANGEL OF ASSASSINATION?

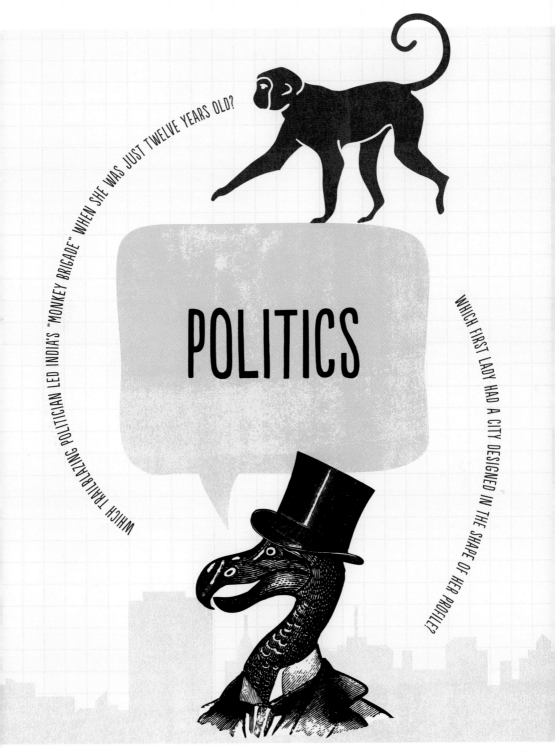

WHICH TRAILBLAZING POLITICIAN LED INDIA'S "MONKEY BRIGADE" WHEN SHE WAS JUST TWELVE YEARS OLD?

POLITICS

WHICH FIRST LADY HAD A CITY DESIGNED IN THE SHAPE OF HER PROFILE?

How did a love for cider lead to the first woman being elected mayor in the United States?

When anti-prohibitionist men decided to play a cruel joke on their town's Women's Christian Temperance Union, they inadvertently shattered a glass ceiling, changing the history of American women in politics forever.

Sober Votes

In 1887, women in Kansas attained the right to vote for city officials and run for municipal office, finally having their say about who would preside over local matters. In April of that year, the small town of Argonia was holding its local elections; the role of mayor was on the top of the ballot. This was great news for the Women's Christian Temperance Union (WCTU). One of the group's political goals was the prohibition of alcohol, but protesting outside saloons had only resulted in members getting abused and dowsed with beer. With the elections coming up, the women seized their chance to vote for someone who would be sympathetic to their cause.

Botched Ballot Papers

At this time, candidates did not register before election day. Instead, campaign groups distributed ballot papers with their preferred list of candidates for supporters to drop in the box at the polling station. The WCTU had selected a list of prohibitionist candidates for the city's important posts. But hard-cider-loving locals, known as "the wets," hatched a plan that they thought would expose the marginal nature of the union's stance, ridiculing the women at the same time. They produced almost identical ballots as the WCTU's, with one exception: They replaced the

> **One of the WCTU's political goals was the prohibition of alcohol.**

male mayoral candidate's name with the name of an enthusiastic WCTU member: Susanna Salter. The idea of a woman mayor was so ludicrous, they thought, only extremists would vote for her.

Mrs. Mayor

But the plan backfired. Salter saw the ballot, and rather than reject the offer to run, she embraced it. Of the 400-strong electorate, 60 percent voted for Salter. The new mayor banned hard cider and served her city for a few years, choosing not to run for re-election. She was the first in a long line of women to be elected to leadership roles in the United States. However, the odds are still stacked against female politicians. In March 2018, just 22 percent of mayors in U.S. cities with populations of more than 30,000 were women.

TEMPERANCE TEMPEST

The WCTU was one of the most influential women's groups of the nineteenth century. Founded in Ohio in 1874, the WCTU's initial focus was prohibition, but members were also instrumental in campaigning for changes in labor laws, prison reform, and women's suffrage. There were more than a thousand local affiliates across the United States, and by the 1920s there were members in more than forty countries. In New Zealand, for example, the WCTU, under Kate Sheppard's leadership, was a dominant force in women being granted universal suffrage in 1893.

Who was the first female prime minister?

On July 22, 1960, Sirimavo Bandaranaike made history when she became the world's first female head of government in the modern world in her home nation of Ceylon, later Sri Lanka. She had only entered politics after the assassination of the country's previous prime minister, her husband, S. W. R. D. Bandaranaike.

A Reluctant Leader

Bandaranaike governed during an important time in her country's history, transforming it into a republic. But initially she was pressured into political life while grieving for her husband, his political party trading on her public sympathy. Sometimes controversially, she carried out her husband's socialist reform strategy and went on to become one of the developing world's best-known leaders. She managed to restore the Sinhalese majority's national dignity after years of British colonialism, although unfortunately this was often at the expense of the Tamil minority. Her coalition government lost the 1965 general election, but she took on the role of prime minister two more times (1970–1977 and 1994–2000). Her daughter would later become the country's first female president.

The Top Job

After Bandaranaike broke down political barriers, a number of other notable women followed in quick succession—Indira Gandhi became the second female prime minister in 1966 (see page 16), a year after her Sri Lankan counterpart left office for the first time. Here are just some of the other women holding down the top job since.

GOLDA MEIR was the modern state of Israel's fourth prime minister and the third woman to hold a prime ministerial position internationally. She was once described by former Israeli prime minister David Ben-Gurion as "the only man" in his cabinet.

Europe's first female president, and the world's first democratically elected female president, was **VIGDÍS FINNBOGADÓTTIR** from Iceland. Despite a shaky start, she became hugely successful, serving for sixteen years from 1980 to 1996.

In Asia, **CORAZON AQUINO** became the continent's first female president after the Philippines' 1986 People Power Revolution. Her husband had been an opponent to the authoritarian regime of President Ferdinand E. Marcos and was assassinated three years earlier.

BENAZIR BHUTTO was assassinated in 2007 when she returned to Pakistan to run for office for the third time. She had previously been the country's prime minister from 1988 to 1990 and again from 1993 to 1996. She was the first elected female leader of a Muslim-majority nation.

In 1995 Africa welcomed the continent's first female head of state into power. Liberia's **ELLEN JOHNSON-SIRLEAF** served for twelve years, inheriting a country ravaged by civil war. She was credited with negotiating settlements, lifting sanctions, and rebuilding infrastructure. She received the Nobel Peace Prize in 2011.

ANGELA MERKEL was named *Time* magazine's Person of the Year in 2016 (one of only four women to have been singled out for the title at the time of writing). She became Chancellor of Germany in 2005—the first woman to do so—and has been the President of the European Council. She's the current longest-serving head of government in the EU.

Which trailblazing politician led India's "Monkey Brigade" when she was just twelve years old?

In 1966 Indira Gandhi became India's first female prime minister at the age of forty-eight, but she got started in politics much younger. Her father, Jawaharlal Nehru, was a leader in the fight for India's independence, so she grew up immersed in the nationalist movement.

Adolescent Activism

At just twelve years old, Gandhi was frustrated that she was too young to join the Congress Party, of which her father would be elected leader in 1929. She launched Vanar Sena (the Monkey Brigade)—a nationalist group for young people.

The name comes from the epic poem *Ramayana* in which an army of monkeys helps the hero, Rama, to conquer the demon king. Initially, Gandhi's parents were just amused by her enthusiasm, but when 1,000 young revolutionaries turned up to the first meeting, they realized that her idea had potential. Soon enough, the children served an important role in the campaign for independence, and the group grew to include 60,000 members. They sewed flags, wrote letters for illiterate imprisoned freedom fighters, and administered food and first aid to

behind her, but that didn't stop her from helping her father out—she routinely served as his travel companion and hostess at diplomatic events, a role that prepared her well later on for her own years in power.

Congress volunteers injured by police. They also conveyed warning messages to freedom fighters who were about to be arrested. As their leader, Gandhi delivered some of her first speeches.

Preparing for Power

In many ways, despite her enthusiasm for politics, Gandhi's teenage years were sad. She had no siblings, a father who was in and out of prison because of his political views, and a mother who died tragically of tuberculosis when she was just eighteen. By then she'd spent a number of years living abroad—first at a Swiss boarding school and then at Oxford University in England. But she never lost sight of her childhood goal: to join the Congress Party, which she did in 1938. Nine years later, she saw her father become the first prime minister of independent India. Her Monkey Brigade days may have been long

NO RELATION

Indira Gandhi shares the same surname as one of India's most important figures, activist Mahatma Gandhi, but the two are not related—Gandhi is a common name in India. While Indira's father was a close associate of Mahatma's, she got her famous surname after she married Feroze Gandhi, whom she had met when he joined the Monkey Brigade.

Who was the Angel of Assassination?

On July 13, 1793, Charlotte Corday, a twenty-four-year-old noblewoman, knocked on the door of outspoken French Revolutionary leader Jean-Paul Marat. She had come to his house to kill him, and she had a knife tucked in the folds of her dress.

The Reign of Terror

The French Revolution (1789–1799) saw the country's commoners overthrow the monarchy and take control of government. Revolutionary leader Marat was a Deputy of Paris

to the newly formed National Convention and he published *L'Ami du Peuple* (*The Friend of the People*)—a propagandist journal that helped fuel the flames of 1793's Reign of Terror, the revolution's bloodiest period. As a moderate republican, and the daughter of an aristocrat, Corday supported a peaceful revolution and constitutional government. Marat epitomized everything she despised about the direction her country was heading.

Bloody Bath Time

After being turned away from Marat's home twice, she persisted, promising to reveal the names of fellow moderates, who Marat saw as "enemies of the revolution." Corday had already settled her debts and written her farewell letters—she knew that if she succeeded, her own fate would be sealed and that there was no turning back. The promise of information was enough to convince Marat to grant her an audience. But the powerful man she had come to loathe was on his last legs—an incurable skin disease meant he had to spend most of his time soaking in a bathtub of medicinal herbs. His skin was rotting with open lesions and he wore a turban around

his head and a linen sheet draped across his shoulders. He sat with a writing table across the tub so he could still attend to business.

As requested, Corday sat in a chair beside the bath as she recited the names of her allies, inadvertently signing their death warrants. And then she rose up and plunged the knife into Marat's chest. He is said to have died almost instantly. Marat received a martyr's funeral: a procession through the streets of Paris and a burial at the Pantheon. Corday, on the other hand, faced a swift trial and was convicted and sentenced to death. Four days after she'd attempted to bring peace to the revolution by a swift act of violence, she lost her own head at the guillotine. In 1847, historian Alphonse de Lamartine nicknamed her the Angel of Assassination.

DEATH ON CANVAS

The Death of Marat by Jacques-Louis David has become one of the French Revolution's most enduring images. David was the Jacobin movement's official artist and a National Convention deputy. He knew Marat well, having visited him in that very bathroom the day before his death, and was asked to paint the murder as part of a propaganda campaign a few months after the event. The painting helped to cement Marat's standing as a revolutionary martyr. While much of what the painting depicts is believed to be accurate—the bathtub, the sheets, Marat's turban—David chose not to include Corday in the image and left out the victim's skin condition, preferring to paint him as a beautiful corpse, in the tradition of religious paintings.

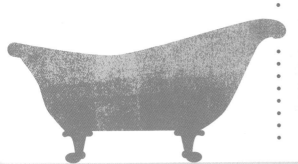

Who were "The Butterflies" and why were they assassinated?

Rafael Trujillo ruled over the Dominican Republic for thirty-one years. Atrocities of his brutal regime included the slaughter of some 20,000 Haitian people in 1937. But an underground movement was determined to oust him from power. Leading the fight were three sisters known as "The Butterflies"—their real names: Patria, Minerva, and Maria Teresa Mirabal.

Las Hermanas Mirabal

The Mirabal sisters were raised in a middle-class farming family, receiving a good education—the three activists earned college degrees in the 1940s. Minerva was the first to oppose Trujillo openly. She snubbed his romantic advances multiple times with dire consequences. She was denied a law license and her father was imprisoned and tortured.

Soon her sisters joined her, and they started the Movement of the 14th June, named for the day Patria witnessed a massacre of anti-Trujillo revolutionaries. They united the middle class against Trujillo, distributing pamphlets to educate the masses about his atrocities. Together with their supportive husbands they were routinely imprisoned, but incarceration only fueled their determination.

Mirabal Murders

Sadly, on November 25, 1960, on returning from visiting their husbands in prison, they were intercepted by Trujillo's police force. The women were beaten to death and their vehicle was pushed off a cliff to make it look like an accident. Their murders were the final straw for many Dominicans, and Trujillo was assassinated six months later. A fourth sister, Dedé, who was not as radical as her sisters, raised their children and ran the Mirabal Sisters Museum in their memory.

Did British Prime Minister Margaret Thatcher help to develop Mr. Whippy ice cream?

Before she entered the political sphere, Margaret Roberts was an Oxford University chemist, who studied X-ray crystallography under Nobel-Prize-winning chemist Dorothy Hodgkin. After graduating she took a job as a chemical researcher and then in 1949 she joined the food research team at J. Lyons & Co.

Whipped Up

It was the same year that she became Mrs. Thatcher and a parliamentary candidate. The story goes that part of her job at Lyons was devising a method for whipping extra air into ice cream, research that formed the foundation for the creation of soft-serve. While there is evidence to show soft-serve was first invented in the United States (some reports say ten years before Thatcher started working for Lyons in the United Kingdom), there's no denying the future Iron Lady started her career on a much sweeter note. During her time with the company, Lyons was trying to develop a recipe similar to the American Softee brand. But it was

another British brand, T. Wall & Sons (Wall's), that would go on to purchase the Mr. Whippy name synonymous with soft-serve in the United Kingdom and around the world.

A Load of Cold Air

Thatcher continued to work as a J. Lyons researcher until 1951. She won a seat in Parliament in 1959 and became Britain's first woman prime minister in 1979. The soft-serve story became a favorite of leftists who joked about Thatcher's role in adding air to ice cream to lower its quality and raise profits—something they felt was symbolic of her leadership.

Who was behind the anti-Nazi leaflets of the White Rose?

In 1942, when Sophie Scholl discovered that her brother Hans was part of an underground Nazi-resistance group, she was shocked, but her shock soon turned to support as she joined him in his fight to wake up the German people to the Nazis' crimes.

Life Under Hitler

Their father, Robert Scholl, a former small-town mayor who worked as a tax and business consultant, was a staunch opponent of Hitler's National Socialist Party. He raised his six children to be open-minded and to question what was going on around them as life grew more and more oppressive. Despite Robert's efforts, Hans had joined the Hitler Youth, becoming a squad leader, while Sophie, along with her sisters, were members of the League of German Girls. It was an exciting time for young people— wearing uniforms, parading in the streets, camping out with friends, and being part of rebuilding their nation and its national pride. But a few years later, they too had become disillusioned with the National Socialist approach—the Scholls were not willing to conform.

The White Rose

In May 1942, while the Nazis were deporting Jewish people en masse to concentration camps, twenty-one-year-old Sophie joined Hans at the University of Munich to study biology and philosophy. But her studies soon took a backseat. Hans, together with four other students, had started a resistance campaign and was distributing anti-Nazi literature. They called themselves The White Rose. When Sophie discovered her brother was behind the leaflets, she wanted in. The group produced five more leaflets, printing them in bulk and taking them by train to neighboring towns across Germany, to evade detection. They also

graffitied phrases like "Down with Hitler" and "Freedom" on Munich's city hall and other public places to get more attention for their cause.

And it worked. When Local Nazi Party boss Paul Giesler, who was against higher education for women, delivered a speech at Munich University on January 13, 1943, students protested and were arrested.

High Risk, High Treason

The White Rose printed another 1,300 leaflets. On February 18, Hans and Sophie were spotted distributing their sixth leaflet on the Munich University campus by a janitor and member of the Nazi Party. They were arrested by the Gestapo alongside fellow White Rose member Christoph Probst. A lengthy interrogation followed, during which they refused to give up their accomplices, and soon after the three of them were charged with high treason. Their trial, held at the People's Court and presided over by Judge Roland Freisler, took place on February 22. They were denied legal representation, and the trial lasted just one hour. There was little hope of justice being done—90 percent of cases that went before the People's Court resulted in the death penalty or life imprisonment. And the White Rose members' fate was no different. All three were sentenced to death and sent to the guillotine a few hours later. Among Sophie's last recorded words, she said: "It is such a splendid sunny day, and I have to go… What does my death matter if by our acts thousands are warned and alerted."

Which First Lady had a city designed in the shape of her profile?

Eva Perón, better known as "Evita," was no ordinary First Lady. Even before her husband, Juan Domingo Perón, came to power in Argentina she had broken gender stereotypes by campaigning alongside him. She became the most powerful woman in the country and, despite not being officially elected, exerted influence over the Ministries of Health and Labor and in new social building projects.

Spiritual Leader of the Nation

Eva had come from a poor family in rural Argentina and moved to the capital as a teenager to pursue an acting career. But these humble beginnings didn't stop her from getting involved in politics once her husband was in power. She oversaw the development of a range of architectural projects, including the construction of 25,000 low-cost homes for working-class families and subsidized grocery stores, and the General San Martin Working Women's Home, which provided safe and comfortable accommodation for 500 female residents. She set up the Eva Perón Foundation and the Female Perónist Party to campaign for better conditions for workers and the poor, as well as for women's rights. Shortly before her death in 1952, the Argentine Congress gave her the title "Spiritual Leader of the Nation."

Ciudad Evita

One of the ultimate expressions of Peronism was with the construction of Ciudad Evita, a suburb of Buenos Aires built by presidential decree in 1947. As if it wasn't enough to name the new residential neighborhood after the First Lady, the development's layout was designed to represent Eva's profile. The one hundred square-foot workers' city is made up of California-esque bungalows typical of Eva's other housing projects. The development has been added to since, but the outline of Perón's face and signature chignon bun can still be seen in aerial photographs of the network of communities. The city was renamed twice in the years after a military coup overthrew the president in 1955, but it has since had its original name reinstated. In 1997, it was declared a National Historical Monument and is now home to some 70,000 people.

Here it is, My Sisters!

Eva Perón is perhaps most well-known for the speech she delivered on September 23, 1947, from the balcony of the Casa Rosada in Buenos Aires, declaring to the crowds below: "Here it is, my sisters!" She was referring to a new law that had just been approved by the National Congress and signed by her husband. It gave Argentine women the same political rights as men—the right to vote and the right to be elected to office. While her husband was in power, Eva was influential in the country's fight for women's suffrage, and this monumental change was a culmination of that effort. Many encouraged her to run for vice president with her husband, but her ill health coupled with opposition from the country's military, prevented her from doing so. Despite Eva's popularity, there were some who felt her feminism was a political strategy to help her husband win votes, which he did when four million women, including his wife, went to the ballot boxes for the first time in 1951, securing him a second presidential term.

How did Washington's Petticoats almost bring down a presidency?

When former tavern maid and widow Margaret "Peggy" Timberlake married her second husband, John Eaton, in 1829, she was probably unprepared for the impact it would have on Washington society at large and Andrew Jackson's presidency.

Notes on a Scandal

Peggy's father ran a popular Washington boarding house and tavern, so she grew up in the company of the country's political elite, socializing with men and engaging in conversation considered unseemly for a woman of the era.

Her marriage to Senator Eaton came shortly after the death of her first husband, navy purser John Timberlake. The wives of Washington were scandalized—rumors swirled that the precocious Peggy and Eaton had been having an affair, which had led Timberlake to commit suicide. Rather than welcome the new cabinet member's wife into their social circle, the women, led by Vice President John C. Calhoun's wife, Floride, shunned her. The "Petticoats" did this in the simplest way possible: They refused to call on her—the ultimate social snub of the day.

Close to Home

The president was furious. He called a cabinet meeting to command that the wives desist and embrace the new couple. But with the exception of Secretary of State Martin Van Buren, a widower who sided with Jackson, there was considerable resistance. When Jackson decided to make Eaton his Secretary of War, he was advised not to because of Peggy's reputation. "Do you suppose that I have been sent here by the people to consult the ladies of Washington as to the proper persons to compose my cabinet?" he is reported to have said. It was not long before he dissolved the entire cabinet—with many of the men who sided with their wives sent to posts far from Washington.

Jackson took the treatment of the Eatons personally, and he had good reason to. Before his election to the presidency, his own marriage to Rachel Robards was the scandal du jour. Robards had been in the process of divorcing her previous husband when she married Jackson, and when he ran for president, this messy marital situation was used as ammunition by the opposition. It was at this time that Rachel's health declined—she had an illness that centered around her heart and lungs. It's thought the stress and depression caused by the campaign worsened her condition. And when she died, three weeks before her husband was elected, he blamed his opponents for her demise.

Divisions that Endured

The impact of the Petticoat Affair was long-lasting. While Eaton resigned from office in 1831, moving to Spain with Peggy to serve as a minister in Madrid, Van Buren's loyalty was rewarded. Jackson chose him over Calhoun as his running mate in 1832 and supported Van Buren's own successful presidential campaign in 1836. The distance between the Jackson and Calhoun camps endured—leading to the Nullification Crisis of 1831, when South Carolina, supported by Calhoun, tried to secede from the Union. Jackson's dominance over Calhoun in this matter is thought to have delayed the Civil War by thirty years.

Who exchanged kisses for votes before women could enter the voting booth?

In Britain in 1784, very few people had the right to vote. You had to be a man, a Protestant, and adhere to specific criteria, depending on your borough. But that didn't stop a group of high-profile women taking to the streets of Westminster to canvas for their favorite candidate.

Votes for Fox

Dressed in the blue and buff colors of the Whig party with a foxtail in her hair, Georgiana Cavendish, the Duchess of Devonshire, was one of Charles Fox's most famous and fabulous supporters. Fox was despised by King George III for his politics and

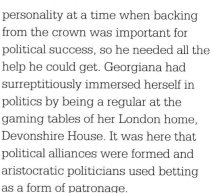

personality at a time when backing from the crown was important for political success, so he needed all the help he could get. Georgiana had surreptitiously immersed herself in politics by being a regular at the gaming tables of her London home, Devonshire House. It was here that political alliances were formed and aristocratic politicians used betting as a form of patronage.

Kissing the Constituents

When it came time to canvas the populace, rather than stay home, Georgiana did the unladylike thing and took to the streets with Fox and a few other wealthy women to champion his cause. Fox's opponents used this against him, ridiculing the duchess in their speeches and comparing her to a prostitute. She was even accused of offering kisses to "an impracticable butcher" and other members of the public in exchange for their votes. True or not, the kisses did the trick, and Fox narrowly secured his seat in the election.

POLITICS

Shoulder pads and stump speeches can't protect you now. It's time to get political and see how much you've remembered.

Questions

1. Iceland's Vigdís Finnbogadóttir was the world's first what?

2. What did Margaret Thatcher study at Oxford University?

3. Which influential women's group was Kansas mayor Susanna Salter a part of?

4. Who was famously left out of Jacques-Louis David's painting The Death of Marat?

5. In which city will you find Ciudad Evita?

6. What did Floride Calhoun famously refuse to do?

7. Georgiana Cavendish was accused of offering what to "an impracticable butcher"?

8. Which Dominican leader did the Mirabal sisters revolt against?

9. Which Hitler Youth group was Sophie Scholl a part of for a time?

10. What was the name of India's twentieth-century nationalist group for young people?

Turn to page 212 for the answers.

WHAT DO YOUR STOCKINGS SAY ABOUT YOUR FEMINIST CREDENTIALS?

WHO SET UP INDIA'S FIRST SCHOOL FOR GIRLS?

WHO WAS ROSIE THE RIVETER?

WHAT DO TENNIS BALLS HAVE TO DO WITH THE BATTLE OF THE SEXES?

FEMINISM

WHICH COUNTRY HAS THE SMALLEST GENDER GAP IN THE WORLD?

What do your stockings say about your feminist credentials?

In eighteenth-century Britain, it was unfashionable for a woman to be educated, and there were few opportunities for formal learning—it wasn't until 1868 that the University of London became the first in the world to admit women. For London's female intelligentsia, this was simply not good enough, and an educational society was born.

The Bluestocking Philosophers

Beginning in the 1750s, during the aristocratic social season, high-born women began assembling in the lavish London homes of literary hostesses—most notably Elizabeth Montagu, Frances Boscawen, and Elizabeth Vesey—to discuss their reading over cups of tea. Chairs were often arranged in a semicircle, in the style of a Parisian salon, with the hostess directing a communal conversation. The meetings also served as networking and patronage opportunities for artists and writers. And it wasn't just women in attendance. A number of men, such as critic and writer Samuel Johnson and actor David Garrick, were also regulars. It was a man, botanist Benjamin Stillingfleet, who showed up one day in blue woolen stockings, considered informal work wear, as opposed to the white silk stockings more typical for an aristocratic social event. The acceptance of Stillingfleet's stockings, and the group's informal adoption of the name "the Bluestockings," was indicative of the egalitarian and

A NEW LITERARY PUBLICATION

While not strictly a feminist society, the original Bluestocking group helped to encourage women to read and discuss ideas, and it made the notion of an educated woman less abhorrent to the aristocracy. Many years later, at the height of the first-wave feminist movement, the name became the title of a Japanese magazine. *Seitō* (*Bluestocking*), was founded by the feminist Bluestocking Society and ran from 1911 to 1916. The magazine translated and published women's literature from around the world, including influential writers and suffragists like Emma Goldman and Ellen Key. It was a radical publication at a time when women still had few rights in a fiercely patriarchal Japan.

eccentric nature of these meetings and the people who attended them. For a while, all the guests were nicknamed "blues" or "Bluestockings," but by the 1770s, this term was more exclusively used to refer to women intellectuals, whether or not they had attended the original meetings. And the name spread—by the nineteenth century there were "Bluestockings" all over Europe.

Painting the Town Red

The second-wave feminist movement of the late 1960s and 1970s saw women meeting once again, this time in large numbers, to discuss feminist ideas and to organize protests. In the United States, younger members of groups like the New York Radical Women felt the legislative change being sought by the National Organization for Women was out of touch with their ideals. The Redstockings (red being the color of revolution) were an offshoot of this group, firmly committed to action-based feminism. Organized by Shulamith "Shulie" Firestone and Ellen Willis, they made their first public appearance at a New York abortion law reform hearing in 1969, where fourteen out of fifteen medical and psychiatric experts were men. The next month they held their own abortion speak-out where women shared their personal experiences in front of an audience. The group is now a grassroots think tank working on women's liberation issues.

What do tennis balls have to do with the Battle of the Sexes?

In 1973, retired U.S. tennis champion Bobby Riggs publically declared men's tennis was so superior to the women's game that he could beat any of the current top female players. The gauntlet had been thrown down. It was Billie Jean King who picked it up.

The First Battle

The exhibition match became known as the Battle of the Sexes and took place on September 20 at the Astrodome in Houston, Texas. But it wasn't the first match where Riggs had taken on a female component in a bid to prove his sex's sporting prowess. King was ranked the number one female player in 1972, but it was the 1973 champion, Margaret Court, who took on Riggs first. Just a few months before the Battle of the Sexes, in a match that earned the title "The Mother's Day Massacre," Riggs beat Court in two sets (6–2, 6–1). Riggs spent up to six hours a day practicing in the build-up to the match, and was on a strict nutritional regime, taking 415 vitamins per day. It was a humiliating defeat for women's tennis and served to prove Riggs' point. This chauvinistic arrogance spurred King on to accept his challenge.

Serving Equality

With $100,000 of prize money and the reputation of women's tennis on the line, King used the publicity generated from the upcoming match with Riggs to make some noise about the inequality of the game.

She organized a meeting in London a week before Wimbledon with more than sixty female players, which led to the establishment of the Women's Tennis Association—the organizing body for women's professional tennis. King also threatened to boycott the 1973 U.S. Open if the male and female champions were not awarded the same amount of prize money. Her demand was met—a first for a major tennis tournament.

Winning the War

The match was a sporting spectacle— King was brought out on a litter carried by shirtless men, while Riggs arrived in a rickshaw surrounded by scantily clad women. King refused to play if disparaging tour promoter Jack Kramer was in the commentary box, so ABC fired him on the spot. Riggs played the first three games wearing his Sugar Daddy jacket to cash in on a sponsorship deal. But when the tennis got going, it was a one-woman show. King obliterated Riggs in straight sets, 6–4, 6–3, 6–3, to the relief of feminists everywhere.

EYES ON THE BALL

On the day of the Riggs vs. King match, 30,472 people took their seats in the stadium. It was the largest live audience ever to attend a tennis match, and held the record for thirty-seven years. (It was broken in 2010 when 35,681 spectators watched Kim Clijsters defeat Serena Williams at King Baudouin Stadium in Brussels, Belgium.) It was given a prime-time television slot, and it's thought some 50 million Americans and 90 million people around the world tuned in to watch it on TV, making it one of the most-watched televised sporting events of all time.

Which country has the smallest gender gap in the world?

In 2017, Iceland topped the World Economic Forum's Global Gender Gap Index for the ninth time. The index measures gender parity in 144 countries, taking into consideration economic participation and opportunity, educational attainment, health and survival, and political empowerment. With some of the world's big economic players like the United States (49th in 2017), Russia (71st), and China (100th) ranking far lower, there's a lot to be learned from this little feminist country.

Legislating Equality

Despite equal pay legislation being in place there since 1961, in 2017 Iceland upped the ante, bringing in a new law that required companies and government agencies to prove they are paying men and women equally. (At that time, Iceland had a gender pay gap of 5.7 percent, compared to 18 percent in the United States.) The new legislation came in the wake of public protests in 2016 when women walked out of their jobs to protest the continuing discrepancy. They were following in the footsteps of the

WOMEN ARE WELCOME

Iceland has a strong feminist tradition—women were granted suffrage in 1915, and in 1980 the country voted in the world's first democratically elected female president. In 2016, women made up 48 percent of elected representatives in Iceland's parliament, and private companies are required to make sure their executive board is made up of at least 40 percent women.

women's strike on October 24, 1975, in which 90 percent of Icelandic women participated to demand equal pay and fair treatment.

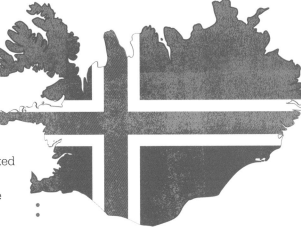

Who set up India's first school for girls?

Often referred to as "the mother of Indian feminism," Savitribai Phule worked tirelessly in nineteenth-century India to fight for the rights of girls and women, as well as against the inhumane and oppressive caste system.

An Education

For centuries, India's hierarchical caste system rigidly divided Hindus into different social groups. Savitribai was born in 1831 in Maharashtra to low-caste parents and received no education. Aged just nine she married thirteen-year-old Jyotirao Phule, whose aunt insisted he attend school despite his similarly low social status. Jyotirao believed girls should be educated, too, so he informally taught his wife at home. Later Savitribai traveled to Pune and Ahmednagar to further her education and train as a teacher—the first woman to do so in India. After her training was complete, the pair opened the country's first girls' school with Savitribai as headmistress in 1848. They would go on to open dozens more schools, including boarding schools for the orphans of the 1875 famine. Savitribai also helped her husband to establish Satyashodhak Samaj, a radical institution that fought for equality of all classes.

Dealing with Discrimination

The couple's other contributions to Indian society are numerous: They established a home for pregnant unmarried women and rape victims; they campaigned against the practice of shaving widows' heads and advocated widow remarriage; they presided over intercaste marriages; and they welcomed society's "untouchables" to drink from their own water tank—something that went against the contemporary notions of purity. Savitribai achieved much in the face of adversity and hostility. In 2014 Savitribai Phule Pune University was named in her honor.

Why did Emily Davison storm the track at Epsom?

On June 4, 1913, the great and the good were gathered at Epsom Racecourse in Surrey, England, for the Derby, a prestigious horse race. The thousands-strong crowd included King George V, Queen Mary, and Emily Wilding Davison—an influential suffragette known for her criminal acts of protest.

The King's Horse

The king's horse, Anmer, was in the running. But as the herd of hoofs rounded the famous Tattenham Corner, heading for the final straight in front of the Royal Box, Anmer was third from last. He was ridden by Herbert Jones, who was wearing the king's colors, making him easy to spot. That was when the unthinkable happened. A woman stepped from behind the protective barrier, out onto the track.

She was holding the suffragette flag, and for a split second she stood in front of Anmer in an act of silent protest, before he charged into her. The horse, Jones, and Davison lay on the ground before Anmer got up and made his way, alone, to the finish line.

Deeds not Words

That day at the Derby was not Davison's first foray into extreme activism. She had quit her job as a teacher to commit herself full-time to the Women's Social and Political Union, a militant offshoot of the National Union of Women's Suffrage Societies founded by Emmeline Pankhurst. She organized and carried out a number of actions, including hiding in the air ducts in the House of Commons to listen in on parliamentary sessions; setting fire to London post

boxes; and throwing metal balls labelled "Bomb" through windows. She was sent to prison numerous times where she had her cell flooded, underwent hunger strikes in protest, and endured torturous force-feeding techniques.

Dying for a Cause

Jones suffered broken ribs and a concussion, but he was back riding again in no time. Davison died from severe internal injuries four days after the incident. The king's mother, Queen Alexandra, wrote to Jones to wish him well, declaring Davison "a brutal lunatic woman," and her actions were widely seen as those of a mentally ill fanatic. People assumed she was trying to pull the horse to the ground. Today, there is much speculation as to whether she intended to kill herself. In her handbag there was a return train ticket and an invitation to a suffragette meeting that same evening. She also had holiday plans with her sister for the near future.

Recent analysis of the race footage, which was captured on three different cameras, revealed that she was not reaching up to pull Anmer to the ground, but that she was attempting to attach a scarf in the suffragette colors to his bridle. Two flags were found on her body. There are also claims that Davison and other women practiced grabbing horses in a park, prior to the Derby, and that they had drawn straws as to who was going to attend.

What sold out the Walker Theater in Winnipeg in 1914?

The Manitoba Political Equality League was a group of dedicated Canadian activists who wanted to change working conditions for the province's female factory workers. But without the vote it was hard for women to enact real change. On January 28, 1914, after unsuccessfully petitioning Manitoba Premier Sir Rodmond Roblin at the province's legislative assembly the day before, the women staged an evening of topical entertainment at Winnipeg's Walker Theater.

Are You Mocking Me?

The program included suffrage songs, the British play *How the Vote Was Won*, and *A Women's Parliament*, a mock legislature that satirized the province's politicians. Mock parliaments were a particularly Canadian contribution to the universal women's suffrage movement. When McClung and her contemporaries took to the stage in Winnipeg, they were joining a two-decade-long tradition. Mock parliaments were collective creations, performed by the women who wrote them. Other famous mock parliaments had taken place in Ontario and British Columbia, and each was usually preceded by an appeal to the provincial legislature to grant women the right to vote. While the Winnipeg mock parliament was filled with comedy, the seriousness of the occasion was made plain by the pamphlets on sale: They spoke of the importance of the issues surrounding women's suffrage.

Making a Point

The play was staged like a real parliament—two rows of chairs facing each other with the speaker perched on a podium between them. The women "members" dressed in black cloaks and read newspapers in between heckling whoever was taking the floor. They discussed important political issues of the day, such as men's attire, in a satirical take on the dress reform debated in real legislatures, and property reform, with a bill proposed to grant property rights to widowers (a woman at the time had little legal claim to her husband's property on his death).

Nellie McClung had read the closing appeal to the legislative assembly the day before, and was chosen to play the Premier, Sir Rodmond Roblin. She had carefully studied Roblin, and according to one account she expertly mimicked his mannerisms and rhetorical speech style. The parliament led up to the main point of contention—whether men should be allowed the right to vote. McClung cleverly used Roblin's language to make her argument. Where Roblin had argued an increase in divorce rates if women had the vote, McClung did the same for the "male vote." "Oh, no, man is made for something higher and better than voting," she said. "The trouble is that if men start to vote, they will vote too much… When men once get the habit [to vote], who knows where it will end?" she cried to raucous laughter. "It is hard enough to keep them at home now!"

Theatrical Change

The mock parliament had quite an impact, playing to three full houses (two in Winnipeg and one in Brandon), making the suffragists some much-needed cash. Exactly two years after the women made a mockery of Roblin and his contemporaries, Manitoba became the first province to grant women the right to vote and hold office.

"The trouble is that if men start to vote, they will vote too much . . . "

Who was Rosie the Riveter?

In 1943, during World War II, the Westinghouse Electric Corporation commissioned artist J. Howard Miller to create forty-two posters to keep spirits high and reduce absenteeism in its factories, where 8,000 electrical utility components and products were manufactured. Each image was posted on the wall of one of its Midwest plants in the United States for two weeks.

We Can Do It!

On February 15 it was the turn of Rosie the Riveter. The now iconic poster portrayed a brunette woman wearing a red polka-dot headscarf and overalls, rolling up her sleeve. Above her head it reads: "We can do it!" The poster was not widely seen at the time but gained recognition in the 1980s when feminists repurposed it for their own cause. The image gets its name from a 1943 song by The Vagabonds and a wartime painting by Norman Rockwell that earned the title first, which was featured on the cover of the *Saturday Evening Post*. In Rockwell's painting, Rosie also wears a blue work jumpsuit. She's eating a sandwich from a lunchbox that bears her name.

The Real Rosie

Artist Howard Miller never officially said who he based Rosie the Riveter on, but a photograph of a woman at an industrial lathe wearing a polka-dot bandana is widely thought to be the inspiration. In the 1980s, Geraldine Hoff Doyle, who had worked as a metal presser in a factory in 1942, identified herself as the girl in the photo. But in 2016 it was discovered that it was taken at a naval air station in Alameda, California, and that the woman in the picture was actually Naomi Parker Fraley. When her identity was officially confirmed she told reporters, "Victory! Victory! Victory!"

Where in the world did women first win the right to vote?

When it comes to women winning the right to vote around the world, change has been slow. In the United Kingdom, for example, the first women's suffrage bill was put before Parliament in 1832, but universal voting rights for all men and women weren't secured until almost a century later in 1928.

Keeping it Local

Before they won the right to vote in national elections, some women in many countries were able to vote in local elections—such as for municipal councilors and school boards. These local rights were what national suffrage campaigns were built on, and the countries that allowed them were among the first wave to grant universal suffrage. One of the first countries where women were accorded the right to vote in local elections is Sweden, where in 1862 tax-paying widows and spinsters were allowed to cast their ballot. This was shortly followed by local rights being granted in Finland and Bohemia. British widows and spinsters who owned their own property could vote in local elections in 1881.

Votes for Women

All women received municipal suffrage in New Zealand in 1886, and it was there, seven years later in 1893, that the Australasian country became the first nation in the world to grant full suffrage to all women, so they could vote in the colonial legislature. At the same time, New Zealander women were able to run for all elective offices, with the exception of the legislature. New Zealand was followed by Australia (1902) and Finland (1906).

Who asked the question "And ain't I a woman?"

After escaping a life of slavery, Sojourner Truth dedicated the rest of her days to fighting for civil rights, both for women and African-Americans. But out of all the speeches she gave, one phrase resonates the most.

Born into Slavery

Truth was born Isabella Baumfree in 1797. As a slave in Dutch-speaking Ulster County, New York, she was bought and sold four times and endured incredible hardships. She was forced to marry another slave, with whom she had five children. Shortly before New York's Anti-Slavery Law of 1827 came into effect, she ran away and settled in New York City.

She had a religious conversion, changed her name, and became a traveling preacher, abolitionist, and women's rights advocate, giving speeches around the country. She met other leading lights of the abolition and women's rights movements, including Frederick Douglass, Elizabeth Cady Stanton, and Susan B. Anthony.

Unconventional Women

At the 1848 Women's Rights Convention, held in Seneca Falls, New York, a Declaration of Sentiments was drawn up by the attendees—including organizers Lucretia Mott and Elizabeth Cady Stanton. The declaration outlined the injustices American women were facing and called on them to organize

THE WHOLE TRUTH

Surprisingly, Marius Robinson's report didn't mention the phrase "And ain't I a woman?"—a refrain that has become synonymous with Truth's speech and both the women's rights and antislavery movements. It's impossible to know if Truth did say it, although she is said to have approved Robinson's transcript, but when Frances Dana Gage wrote about the convention twelve years after the fact, she chose to repeat the rhetorical question multiple times in her recollection of the speech. "I could work as much as and eat as much as a man, when I could get it, and bear the lash as well. And ain't I a woman?" she recalled. Gage also changed much of the wording and added a Southern slave dialect. Whether Truth said these words or not, her impassioned oration left an indelible mark on history.

themselves and fight for their rights. This galvanized the women of Ohio, and in 1851 Frances Dana Gage led a statewide women's rights convention in Akron. There was a big turnout, but many of the attendees were men who had come to heckle the speakers, one of whom was Truth.

The Speech of her Life

On the second day, male ministers began protesting the women's demands for suffrage, claiming women were weak and undeserving of the vote. But then Truth delivered her rebuttal. "I have as much muscle as any man," said the near six-foot-tall Truth, "and can do as much work as any man. I have plowed and reaped and husked and chopped and mowed, and can any man do more than that?" In *The Anti-Slavery Bugle*, journalist Marius Robinson reported that Truth's speech was one of the most "unique and interesting" of the convention. "It is impossible to transfer it to paper," he said, "or to convey any adequate idea of the effect it produced on the audience."

Why did women march in Pretoria in 1956?

In 1913, the Union of South Africa's Free State introduced a new requirement that black women must carry reference documents on them at all times. Many refused and the rules were soon changed. But when the country's apartheid government tried to reinstate the law years later, they could stay silent no longer. It was time to take to the streets.

Pass Laws Under Apartheid

The Blacks Act No. 67 of 1952 required all black people over the age of sixteen in all provinces to carry a pass or "reference book" at all times. The book had to be signed by the person's employer every month, was a certification of tax payments, and showed whether a person had authorization to be within a particular area.

Women had long been sideline supporters of the anti-apartheid movement. Some groups, like the African National Congress (ANC), had started to admit women members, but there was still a lot of resistance to female involvement—the ANC Women's League wasn't formed until 1948, the same year as the start of apartheid. Initially, female activists, including Lilian Ngoyi, Helen Joseph, and Albertina Sisulu, formed the Federation of South African Women to combat sexism in the movement, but soon their attention turned to the pass law and the 1950 Group Areas Act, which designated different residential neighborhoods to different races.

On that day in 1956 one of the march's leaders was eighteen-year-old Sophia Williams-De Bruyn, who had been an organizer of the Coloured People's Congress in Johannesburg. At the sixtieth anniversary of the march in 2016, Williams-De Bruyn, then seventy-eight, delivered a speech telling young women to be more active in lobbying for their rights. "It's time for the youth to take the baton . . . to fight the ills and the injustices in our country right now, which include the increase in the abuse of women, violence against women and children, and the wage gap."

Solid As a Rock

The women, together with the ANC Women's League, organized a protest march, despite the fact unauthorized gatherings were banned. And on August 9, 1956, 20,000 women of all races marched to the Union Buildings—the official seat of the South African Government—in Pretoria to hand over their petition to the country's prime minister, J. G. Strijdom. As the women walked they sang: *"Wathint' abafazi, wathint' imbokodo, uza kufa!"*—meaning "[When] you strike the women, you strike a rock, you will be crushed [you will die]!"

Fighting for Freedom

It was hailed as one of the most influential demonstrations against the apartheid regime, and 1956 marked the year women became fully and visibly involved in the struggle. Despite the efforts of the women, many of whom faced arrest and criminal prosecution, the apartheid government did nothing. The peaceful approach would soon be usurped by the strikes, boycotts, and civil disobedience of the Pan Africanist Congress. But despite mass bloodshed and armed resistance, including the horrors of the Sharpeville Massacre in 1960, the pass laws wouldn't be repealed until 1986.

Which seminal twentieth-century feminist book was unsuitable for Catholics?

The *Index Librorum Prohibitorum*, meaning "index of forbidden books," was a list of titles once banned by the Roman Catholic church. The list, which dates back to 1559, contained works considered potentially damaging to the morals of the faithful. One of the last books to end up on it was *The Second Sex* by French author Simone de Beauvoir.

Banning Beauvoir

The Second Sex, published in two volumes in 1949, is widely regarded as one of the most influential books of the twentieth century, particularly by the second-wave feminist movement. It was hugely successful, both in France

and abroad, becoming a best seller in its first two weeks of release in the United States. It addressed the treatment of women throughout history, and included de Beauvoir's philosophy on motherhood, economic independence, sexuality, ageing, housework, and abortion. She argued that anti-abortion thinking had more to do with "masculine sadism" toward women than morality, referring specifically to the Catholic church's stance, which probably had a lot to do with the book winding up on the forbidden book index.

Immoral no More?

On June 4, 1966, the Congregation for the Doctrine of the Faith announced in the Vatican newspaper that the index would no longer have any juridical value—it was put in a reliquary and covered with a glass bell. Although Roman Catholics would still be expected to avoid the works on the list, they would not incur any ecclesiastical penalties for reading or distributing the publications. The Holy See, however, reserved the right to condemn publicly any book he felt would be offensive to the faith in the future.

FEMINISM

It's time to cast your hard-earned vote and unleash your factual feminist with this quick quiz.

Questions

1. Who was Nellie McClung impersonating in *A Women's Parliament*?

2. What year did New Zealand women receive full suffrage?

3. What happened at the Mother's Day Massacre in 1973?

4. Which Indian woman had a university named in her honor in 2014?

5. In which American state did Sojourner Truth deliver her famous "And ain't I a woman?" speech?

6. Which famous feminist group were the Redstockings an offshoot of?

7. What was the name of the king's horse the jockey was riding on the day Emily Davison was killed?

8. What did all South African black people over the age of sixteen have to carry to comply with the Blacks Acts of 1952?

9. Who wrote *The Second Sex*?

10. Who painted the original Rosie the Riveter that appeared on the cover of the *Saturday Evening Post*?

Turn to page 212 for the answers.

WHICH FAMOUS AVIATOR HAD HER OWN CLOTHING LINE?

WHO CAME UP WITH THE FIRST EVER COMPUTER PROGRAM?

WHEN DID A WOMAN FIRST CLIMB EVEREST?

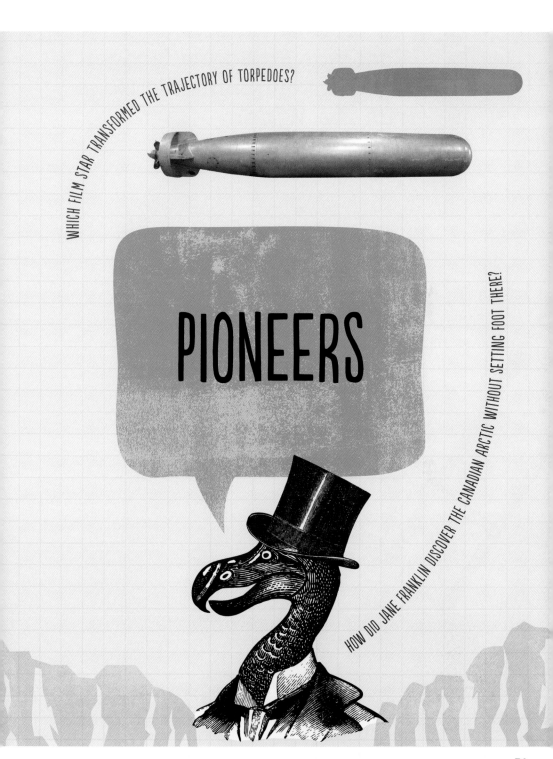

WHICH FILM STAR TRANSFORMED THE TRAJECTORY OF TORPEDOES?

PIONEERS

HOW DID JANE FRANKLIN DISCOVER THE CANADIAN ARCTIC WITHOUT SETTING FOOT THERE?

What was Katharine Blodgett's invisible contribution to *Gone with the Wind*?

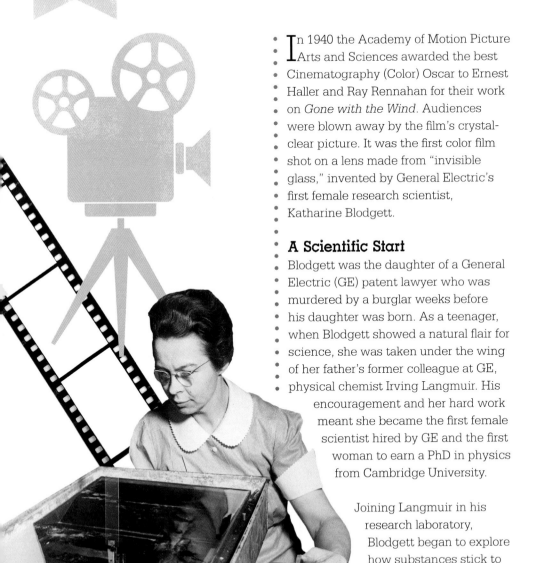

In 1940 the Academy of Motion Picture Arts and Sciences awarded the best Cinematography (Color) Oscar to Ernest Haller and Ray Rennahan for their work on *Gone with the Wind*. Audiences were blown away by the film's crystal-clear picture. It was the first color film shot on a lens made from "invisible glass," invented by General Electric's first female research scientist, Katharine Blodgett.

A Scientific Start

Blodgett was the daughter of a General Electric (GE) patent lawyer who was murdered by a burglar weeks before his daughter was born. As a teenager, when Blodgett showed a natural flair for science, she was taken under the wing of her father's former colleague at GE, physical chemist Irving Langmuir. His encouragement and her hard work meant she became the first female scientist hired by GE and the first woman to earn a PhD in physics from Cambridge University.

Joining Langmuir in his research laboratory, Blodgett began to explore how substances stick to each other on a molecular

level, creating molecule-thick films of oil and other substances on the surface of water. Langmuir won the Nobel Prize for Chemistry in 1932 for the practical application of their work. Blodgett continued the research, adding multiple microscopic layers of oil to both sides of sheets of glass. These Langmuir-Blodgett films, as they were known, were made up of nearly 3,000 single-molecule layers, which canceled out the reflections from the glass surface, making it much easier to see through.

Smashing the Invisible Glass Ceiling

In 1938, Blodgett received a patent for the "film structure and method of preparation" invention. When GE announced the product, they called it "invisible glass." As well as being used for camera lenses and projectors, which all featured invisible glass within a few years, it had a number of other useful applications. In World War II, it appeared in spy cameras for airplanes and periscopes for submarines. And Blodgett's discovery is wide-reaching; nonreflective glass is now used for computer screens, microscopes, eyewear, and car windshields.

Female Intuition

Blodgett also received patents for seven other inventions, including a method for deicing aircraft wings, but she is far from the only woman to turn a clever idea into reality. Here are some other impressive inventors:

STEPHANIE KWOLEK: This American chemist's research into long molecule chains at low temperatures in the 1960s resulted in the invention of Kevlar—a synthetic material five times stronger than steel.

MARIA TELKES: A Hungarian-born physical chemist, Telkes developed a solar-powered thermoelectric generator to heat a building—the world's first solar-powered house.

NANCY JOHNSON: Fans of ice cream in the nineteenth-century had a lot to thank American housewife Johnson for—she devised a hand-cranked ice-cream maker in the time before freezers had been invented.

MARIA BEASLEY: Many more lives would have been lost at sea, especially when the *Titanic* sank, if it wasn't for serial inventor Beasley's life raft—compared to its predecessors, it was fireproof, lightweight, and relatively easy to launch.

When did a woman first climb Everest?

In 1969 when Junko Tabei started the Ladies Climbing Club in Japan, she had an ultimate goal—taking a women-only expedition to the ultimate climbing destination: Everest. Little did she know, a few years later she would become the thirty-sixth person to make the climb and the first woman to reach the summit.

Sexism on the Slopes

At a time when sexism was rife, and Japanese women were expected to be homemakers, Tabei's ambition to climb Everest was ridiculed by her male peers. (The mountain was first summited by Sir Edmund Hillary in 1953.) On her home turf, many men refused to climb with the 4-foot-9 inch mother, which was the impetus for her women-only climbing club. After a successful 1970 expedition to Annapurna III, Tabei and her fellow female climbers (a fifteen-strong group) applied successfully in 1972 for a permit to climb Everest—their dedicated slot was in 1975, and they began their preparations in earnest.

The Japanese Women's Everest Expedition was made up of teachers, a computer programmer, a lawyer, and two mothers (including Tabei, who had a three-year-old daughter at the time). Sponsors were uninterested in funding their trip and told them a women-only expedition was an impossible feat. Eventually, they found enough sponsorship money, contributing much of it themselves—Tabei financed her portion by teaching piano lessons. The team had to cut corners when it came to clothing and equipment: They made their own sleeping bags, collected jam packets from their kids' school lunches for high-sugar snacks, and Tabei even made her waterproof gloves from a car cover.

Tabei might have been the first, but Malavath Purna was the youngest—the Indian girl was only thirteen years and eleven months old when she reached the summit in 2014. Lakpa Sherpa, from Nepal, has reached the summit more times than any other woman. In 2018 she beat her own record when she made her ninth successful ascent.

Women on Top of the World

It was spring 1975 when they started their ascent up the Southeast Ridge route. But on May 4, at 20,670 feet, trouble struck when they were caught in an avalanche. Tabei and two other climbers were trapped in their tent and almost suffocated. Luckily, Tabei was able to pass her penknife to another climber who slashed the tent, and their Sherpas pulled them out. Twelve days later, on May 16, Tabei reached the summit. Because some of the Sherpas were suffering from altitude sickness, and there weren't enough oxygen bottles for all the women to summit, Tabei was chosen by the team's leader to make the final push—and history in the process. Less than two weeks later, Phanthog from Tibet, as part of a Chinese expedition, became the second woman to reach the summit, and the first from the North Face route. Tabei went on to become the first woman to complete the Seven Summits—reaching the highest point on each continent—in 1992.

How did a straw hat make American history?

In the eighteenth century, if an American woman came up with a great invention, she had no way of protecting it. And why would she need to? In a number of states women couldn't legally own any property independently of their fathers or husbands. But the Patent Act of 1790 changed all that.

Patent Genius

Mary Dixon Kies from Connecticut received the first patent granted to a woman by the United States Patent and Trademark Office. Her patent was signed by President James Madison on May 15, 1809. The Patent Act allowed "any person or persons" to protect their original methods and designs.

Dixon Kies had come up with a new technique for weaving straw with silk and thread to make hats—it was cost-effective, and the style soon developed into a fashion trend.

Dixon Kies's technique was a boon to the growing domestic fashion industry. A prohibition on the import of British goods was in place at the time. This was in response to the impressment of American sailors and seizure of sea-faring goods by the British during the Napoleonic Wars. As a result, the government was trying to encourage American manufacturing. Hat making was a vital industry—women wore straw hats to work the fields, and the New England hat trade was thriving. First Lady Dolley Madison personally praised Dixon Kies for her contribution to helping women in manufacturing.

The Last Straw

Sadly, despite her claim to patent law fame, Dixon Kies didn't get rich from her invention. Fashion trends soon changed, and she died penniless. Her final resting place was a pauper's grave. Today, however, there's a fitting monument in her birthplace honoring her significant first for American women.

Who came up with the first ever computer program?

Cambridge mathematics professor Charles Babbage invented the world's first general purpose computer in 1834. But it was a woman who truly understood the machine's capabilities and wrote the first ever computer program.

Analyzing Ada

Babbage first encountered a teenage Ada Lovelace (née Byron, daughter of celebrated Romantic poet Lord George Byron), in 1833. Lovelace took a keen interest in science and math, and the two began a correspondence that would last for years. In 1842, Babbage delivered a lecture about his theoretical invention, the Analytical Engine, which would use punch cards for input and output, at the University of Turin in Italy. The Italian mathematician Luigi Menabrea wrote a paper in French about the machine, and Babbage asked Lovelace, by then in her late-twenties, to translate it.

She did one better, adding her own personal annotations. The English version of the paper, published in 1843, was three times the original's length and included not only her explanatory notes, showing how well she

AHEAD OF HER TIME

Babbage never built the Analytical Engine, but Lovelace's paper mused on its potential uses, such as speeding up complex algebraic calculations, and its role in numerical discoveries. She even touched on the idea of artificial intelligence. Lovelace predicted the future of computing, which was still some one hundred years away. Ada Lovelace Day, an international celebration of women in STEM (science, technology, engineering, and math) industries, is held every year in October.

understood the machine and its workings, but also a groundbreaking algorithm to calculate Bernoulli numbers—a complicated mathematical sequence.

Where did Annie Londonderry go on her bike?

In 1896, social reformer and women's rights activist Susan B. Anthony wrote, "I think [the bicycle] has done more to emancipate women than any one thing in the world." These words came shortly after one woman took that two-wheeled emancipation to a whole new level.

One-Woman Adventure

On June 26, 1894, Annie Cohen Kopchovsky (later changed to Londonderry for publicity reasons), a Latvian-Jewish immigrant and mother of three, left the Massachusetts State House in Boston where a 500-strong crowd had gathered to see her off on an around-the-world adventure. She rode a hefty Columbia bicycle and was wearing a long skirt. She carried a small suitcase and a revolver. She had fifteen months to make it back, checking in at consulates along the way.

Two-Wheeled Wager

Annie's deadline was supposedly imposed by a wager from two Bostonian gentlemen who had bet her $10,000 she wouldn't be able to cycle her way around the world in fifteen months. The wager brought significant publicity to the stunt, and in turn the sponsorship required for such a trip, but it's widely believed that it was a fabrication, and that Annie took on the challenge for the fame and adventure alone (she was not an accomplished cyclist or traveler). At a time when women were still seen as incapable and feeble, the "Battle of the Sexes"-style challenge (see page 34) caught the public's imagination.

After setting off, Annie took a detour to Chicago, where she switched her heavy women's ride for a twenty-one-pound men's Sterling and changed into men's cycling clothes before

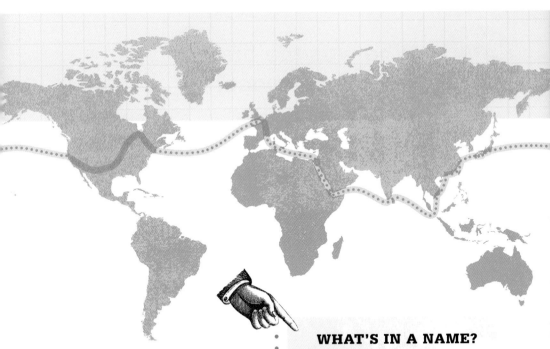

heading to New York and sailing to Le Havre, France. From there she went on through North Africa, the Arabian Peninsula, South and East Asia—traveling by steamer ship where necessary. The total distance she cycled is not known, but it's believed she racked up at least 7,000 miles in the saddle. After docking in San Francisco, she made her way back across the country to officially finish in Chicago on September 12, 1895, fourteen days ahead of schedule.

After the excitement died down, Londonderry moved to New York and briefly wrote a column for the *New York World*, before having a fourth child and resuming the relatively uneventful life of a nineteenth-century wife and mother.

WHAT'S IN A NAME?

If you look up Annie Cohen Kopchovsky in the history books, you're unlikely to find anything. That's because she changed her name to Annie Londonderry to help fund the trip. The Londonderry Lithia Spring Water Company paid her $100 to change her name for the duration of the trip, and her money-making exploits didn't stop there. Annie exaggerated and fabricated all kinds of stories to drum up publicity for the paid lectures and public appearances she made en route—she claimed to be an orphan, an affluent heiress, and an inventor, and she told tales of near-death experiences, meeting royalty, and tousling with Bengal tigers. She also sold advertising space on her clothes and her bike—it's thought that a spot on her left breast pocket went for $100.

Who was the first woman in space?

Two decades before the United States sent a woman, Sally Ride, to space in 1983, the Soviet space program trained five women to become cosmonauts. But only one would sit aboard the *Vostok 6* and become the first woman to leave Earth and enter orbit. Her name was Valentina Tereshkova.

Ready for Anything

The space race was as much a propaganda machine for the United States and the Soviet Union as it was a technological challenge. After the Soviet Union sent the first man to space (Yuri Gagarin in 1961), there were rumors the Americans would try and send a woman. To beat the United States in the race, the Soviets recruited female pilots and parachutists, including Tereshkova, who had written to the Soviet Space Center volunteering herself. Tereshkova came from humble beginnings—her family worked on a collective farm and her father had fought in World War II. She worked in a textile factory and had taken correspondence courses to continue her education. She was also a capable parachutist with 126 jumps to her name. (This skill was essential, as cosmonauts at the time were required to parachute from their capsules before landing.) Together with four other women, she beat 400 hopefuls and traveled to Star City in Moscow Oblast to start training.

Through the Ringer

The women were put through the same intensive training as their male counterparts. They endured high g-force centrifuge training that was much more rigorous than that

SPACE CHILD

Her feet back on terra firma, Tereshkova became a test pilot and instructor, graduating from the Zhukovsky Air Force Engineering Academy. In 1976 she earned a doctorate degree in technical sciences. Shortly after her space flight, she married fellow cosmonaut Andriyan Nikolayev (the third Russian to travel into space). Their daughter, Elena, arrived soon after and earned the title of the first child born to parents who had both been to space—she was of interest to the medical community for a while, and later became a doctor.

undertaken by today's cosmonauts, withstood extreme heat in thermal chambers, and underwent weightless flights, parachute jumps, and isolation tests. After the training was complete, the women were commissioned as lieutenants in the Soviet Air Force.

The Seagull Soars

In 1963 Tereshkova was selected to train for a dual space mission—her call sign was *Chaika*, Russian for seagull. She would be piloting *Vostok 6*, while male cosmonaut Valery Bykovsky would pilot *Vostok 5*. The two spacecraft would take different orbits, pass each other in space, and exchange communications. The mission was a success. After

blasting off on June 16, Tereshkova spent seventy hours and forty-one minutes in space (more than the combined space flight time of all the American astronauts up until then), orbiting the earth forty-eight times before parachuting to land near Karaganda in Kazakhstan. It was her one and only space flight—after a series of tragedies, including the *Soyuz 11* disaster in 1979 when the whole Russian crew died during re-entry, the women cosmonaut program was paused. Another woman wouldn't go to space until Svetlana Savitskaya's *Salyut 7* space station mission in 1982.

Which famous aviator had her own clothing line?

Amelia Earhart is hailed as a feminist icon, an adventurer, and an aviation pioneer, but her brief foray into fashion is less well-known . . .

Taking to the Skies

In the early part of the twentieth century, when universal suffrage and sex discrimination legislation were helping to open doors for many Western women, the world of aviation represented freedom to those with the skills, derring-do, and finances to enter it. Amelia Earhart was a record-setting pioneer—she was the first woman to fly across the Atlantic and the first woman to do it solo. In 1937, she set off on an equatorial round-the-world flight—her second attempt to be the first person to do so. She flew, with navigator Fred Noonan, to Brazil, Dakar, Khartoum, Bangkok, Darwin, and Lae in Papua New Guinea, among other locations.

On July 2 they took off from Lae headed for the small Pacific island of Howland, but never made it. The plane went missing somewhere in the South Pacific and has never been found.

A Different Runway

To fund her flying, Earhart had already become accustomed to press tours and endorsements—she lent her name to the Baltimore Luggage Company, as well as to cigarette and chocolate advertising. In late 1933 Amelia Earhart Fashions launched in thirty department stores in select U.S. cities—it

was thought to be the first celebrity fashion line. The collection of ladies' clothes was made up of twenty-five outfits that could be bought as separates—women could mix and match sizes, an innovation at the time. The designs weren't particularly fashion-forward, but they were intended for a more active woman. Earhart chose fabrics like parachute silk and airplane wing textiles to lend the clothing a more outdoorsy feel. There were propeller-shaped buttons and labels featuring Earhart's signature and a small red plane taking off. Despite being fairly affordable (Earhart also sold the patterns through *Woman's Home Companion* magazine for those who couldn't afford to buy the ready-made versions), the line only lasted one season.

High Fliers

Amelia Earhart may be one of the most well-known female aviators of the early twentieth century, but around the world there were plenty of other women taking to the skies to make a living and a name for themselves. Here are just a few.

HANNA REITSCH: One of the Third Reich's best-known pilots, Reitsch was a Luftwaffe test pilot throughout World War II. She was also the first person to fly a helicopter and the first person to fly a glider over the Alps.

MAUDE BONNEY: Australian aviator Bonney was the first woman to circumnavigate mainland Australia by air, and the first woman to fly solo from Australia to England.

JACQUELINE COCHRAN: An American pilot with more records for speed, altitude, and distance flying than any other pilot, male or female, Cochran was the first woman to break the sound barrier in 1953.

BESSIE COLEMAN: Racial prejudice meant Coleman had to travel to France to learn to fly. There she became the first African American woman to earn a pilot's license in 1921. She was a popular exhibition flyer who performed at air shows across the United States.

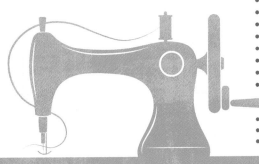

How did Jane Franklin discover the Canadian arctic without setting foot there?

When London-born Jane Griffin married John Franklin at the age of thirty-seven in 1828, she was already a very well-traveled woman by Victorian standards. The daughter of a silk merchant, she'd toured extensively throughout Europe. But when her husband went missing trying to find the Northwest Passage, she inadvertently became a driving force of polar exploration.

Unchartered Territory

In 1845, Sir John Franklin, who had visited the Arctic twice before marrying Jane, took two ships and 129 crew members on an expedition in search of a route through the Canadian Arctic, with the aim of opening up a faster trade passage between Europe and Asia. Franklin planned to be gone a while, but when there was no word after three years,

the British government sent out search parties. But it was to no avail, and they soon slowed their efforts to find the vessels. Jane petitioned the prime minister and the U.S. president to keep looking, before self-funding five of her own missions between 1850 and 1857 to find out what had happened.

News from the Arctic

The explorers aboard Lady Franklin's expeditions made many new discoveries: surveying the west coast of Greenland, recording preciously undocumented plant life, as well as eventually finding the Northwest Passage. Finally, in 1859, Francis Leopold McClintock returned on the *Fox* with a message he'd found buried under a pile of rocks: Sir Franklin had died within a year of the expedition's departure from London. Jane Franklin's passion for discovery and her determination significantly contributed to our knowledge of the Arctic. In 2014 and 2016 the two Franklin ships were finally found, ending over 160 years of searching.

How did Nellie Bly put Phileas Fogg to shame?

Elizabeth Jane Cochran, better known by her pen name Nellie Bly, was one of America's first investigative journalists, putting herself at the center of the story to find out the truth.

Whistle-Stop World Tour

Her most well-known escapade came after she read *Around the World in Eighty Days* by Jules Verne, published in 1873. The hugely popular novel, in which Phileas Fogg embarks on a globe-trotting odyssey, inspired Bly to try and do it in seventy-five days. She traveled light, without a single spare dress, and ventured off to Europe, then Egypt, Singapore, Hong Kong, and back via San Francisco. She even had time to make a detour to Amiens, France, to meet Jules Verne himself. She arrived back in New Jersey on January 25, 1890, taking three days less than she'd planned. Unbeknownst to Bly, Elizabeth Bisland, a rival journalist for *Cosmopolitan* magazine, had been racing against her, traveling in the opposite direction. Bisland made it back four and a half days later.

Ten Days in the Madhouse

After working in her first journalism job as a columnist for the *Pittsburgh Dispatch*, Nellie Bly moved to New York and stormed into the offices of the *New York World*. She wanted to write about the immigrant experience, but the editor set her the challenge of writing about one of New York's most notorious mental hospitals instead. She took the bull by the horns and had herself admitted to the Women's Lunatic Asylum on Blackwell's Island. Her ten days spent at the facility were covered in a six-part series and earned her national recognition.

Which film star transformed the trajectory of torpedoes?

Until recently, Hedy Lamarr was known as little more than a Hollywood starlet who looked good and married frequently, famous for her roles in Oscar-nominated films of the 1940s like *Algiers* and *Sampson and Delilah*. But it was her contribution to technology that had the biggest impact on society.

Austrian Beauty

Born in Vienna, Austria, in 1934, Hedy Lamarr fled to England to escape an unhappy marriage to munitions manufacturer Fritz Mandl. After meeting MGM studio head Louis B. Mayer in London, she traveled to Beverly Hills to pursue her acting career. Her striking looks landed her a contract with the studio, although they struggled to find suitable roles for her—she spoke little English and her reputation (see box) meant the studio struggled to manage her public image. She got her big break in *Algiers* and went on to star in *Lady of the Tropics*, *Boom Town*, and *Come Live with Me*, among others.

Tinkering on Set

Her beauty might have been the main focus in front of the cameras, but in between takes Lamarr was putting her brain to work. She was an enthusiastic tinkerer, who was always inventing something in her home laboratory. She even had some equipment (reportedly provided by businessman and engineer Howard Hughes, whom she briefly dated) set up in her trailer so she could

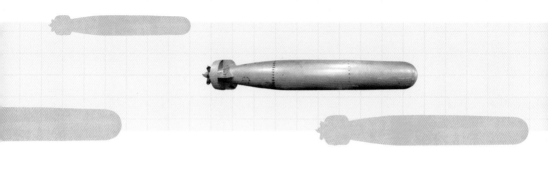

work on her experiments in her downtime. Hughes encouraged Lamarr's hobby, and even took her advice when she suggested he redesign the square wings of his planes to better reflect the wings and fins of fast birds and fish.

ORGASMIC FIRSTS

Science may have been her passion, but it was a passionate performance by Lamarr in the 1933 arthouse flick *Ecstasy* that really got her noticed. In the picture, by Czech filmmaker Gustav Machatý, Lamarr, who then went by her birth name Hedwig Kiesler, played a frustrated bride who leaves her husband and meets a new man. In one scene Lamarr performs what many believe is the first simulated female orgasm captured on film. The movie was criticized by the pope and was banned in the United States. That didn't stop illicit screenings and the actress being known as "The Ecstasy Girl" for most of her career.

In 1942, in the middle of World War II, Lamarr, together with composer George Antheil, was granted a patent for a "Secret Communication System." Though some think it was inspired by her first husband Mandl's work or blueprints she'd seen in his office, it was to be Lamarr's most significant invention. The pair had figured out a coded form of radio communication, using "frequency hopping" to help guide torpedoes to their targets without being detected and to prevent classified messages from being intercepted by the enemy. This technology would have been invaluable to the Allied forces. As it turned out, the patent wasn't used until much later, during the Cold War, on U.S. Navy ships during the Cuban Missile Crisis. Lamarr and Antheil's patent underpins the array of wireless technology we use today, from Wi-Fi to GPS tracking.

Who invented *Monopoly?*

It's widely accepted that Charles Darrow was the Depression-era inventor of the Parker Brothers' hugely successful board game *Monopoly*. The story goes that he was down on his luck, then struck upon the idea and sold it, making millions in the process. But it was actually Elizabeth Magie, a Washington-based stenographer who came up with the game.

Take a Chance

In 1903, decades before *Monopoly* appeared on toy store shelves, Magie filed a patent for *The Landlord's Game*. It was based on the theories of anti-monopolist politician Henry George, who believed that land should belong to everyone. Magie's game could be played in two different ways: the antimonopolist version, in which all players were rewarded when wealth was created, and the monopolist version whereby the aim was to beat your opponents and create monopolies. Unusually for the time, her game featured a path that circled the board. Printed on Magie's game were those dreaded words: "Go to Jail." She intended for the game to be a teaching tool to demonstrate that the anti-monopolist approach was better, but it was the latter version that appealed to the masses.

Do not Pass Go

Magie's game was especially popular in the American Northeast. A group of Quakers in Atlantic City adapted the board with their neighborhood's names and added prices. They also simplified the rules. This is the game that Charles Darrow eventually sold to Parker Brothers. While he became a millionaire, Magie is thought to have made just $500, and her name is largely forgotten.

PIONEERS

Thirsty for adventure? On a quest for knowledge?
Put your nerves to the test with these pioneering
questions.

Questions

1. Why did Annie Cohen Kopchovsky change her name?
2. What was Valentina Tereshkova's call sign?
3. Who invented the world's first solar-powered house?
4. What did Mary Dixon Kies's patented technique allow you to do?
5. Who was Lord Byron's famous computer-programming daughter?
6. What innovative change did Amelia Earhart Fashions make to the way outfits were sold?
7. What did Hedy Lamarr receive a patent for?
8. What was Elizabeth Magie's board game called?
9. Who finished traveling around the world a few days after Nellie Bly?
10. What did Junko Tabei use to make waterproof gloves for her Everest expedition?

Turn to page 213 for the answers.

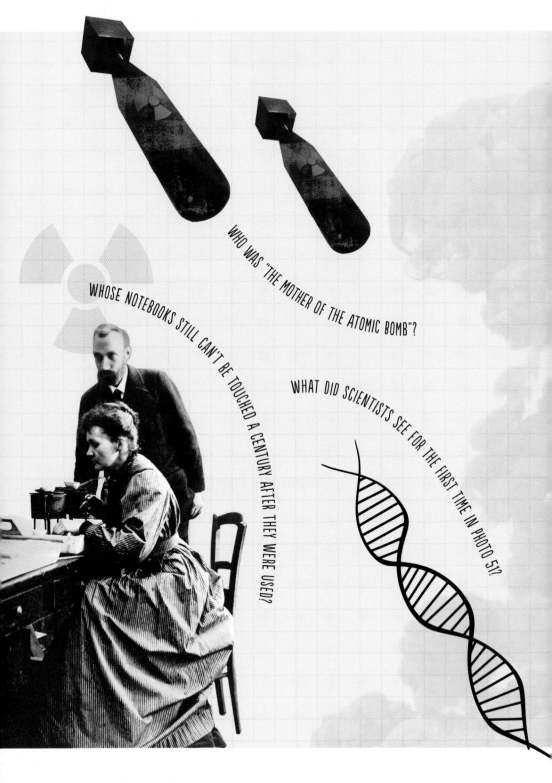

WHO WAS "THE MOTHER OF THE ATOMIC BOMB"?

WHOSE NOTEBOOKS STILL CAN'T BE TOUCHED A CENTURY AFTER THEY WERE USED?

WHAT DID SCIENTISTS SEE FOR THE FIRST TIME IN PHOTO 51?

WHO WAS THE FIRST WOMAN TO EARN A UNIVERSITY DEGREE?

THINKERS

HOW DID A NURSE CHANGE THE WAY POLIO WAS TREATED?

Whose notebooks still can't be touched a century after they were used?

Marie Curie was known to walk around with bottles of polonium in her coat pocket. She kept radium in her desk drawer. It's no wonder, then, that her notebooks still can't be touched with bare hands—and won't be for some time to come.

• Radioactive Research

Visitors to the Biblothèque nationale de France in Paris who want to look at some of the country's extensive historical collections might expect to wear gloves or view works in specially designed rooms to protect ageing papers from damage. But for those interested in checking out the Pierre and Marie Curie Collection of manuscripts and other possessions, it's the visitors who need protecting. Donning special clothing and signing a liability waiver is required, because the scientists' notebooks, as well as their furniture and cookbooks, are contaminated with the radioactive element radium 226. They're even stored in lead-lined boxes, just in case. Radium 226 has a half-life of 1,601 years—that means that even over one hundred years after the Curies handled these objects, they still have more than a millennium to go before the radiation levels are halved.

Curious Curie

Marie Curie, together with her husband and work partner Pierre, were researching the invisible rays given off by uranium at the Sorbonne's school of chemistry and physics in Paris when they discovered two new much more radioactive chemical elements: polonium (which they named after Marie's home country of Poland) and radium. To isolate a sample of radium, Curie had to process large quantities of pitchblende, an industrial waste product from uranium extraction. The material would be ground, dissolved, filtered, and precipitated, before collection and crystallization could take place. All this work was physically demanding—particularly since both Curie and her husband were suffering from radiation sickness caused by exposure to the radioactive elements they were handling on a daily basis. They were unaware of the short- and long-term risks of radiation—at the time many people assumed the powerful energy was beneficial, and manufacturers used radioactive minerals in toothpaste, bath salts, and drinking vessels.

Lead and Buried

Arguably, their hard work paid off. They were awarded the Nobel Prize for Physics in 1903. While Pierre died in a tragic road accident in 1906, Marie continued to be a radiation pioneer, receiving a second Nobel Prize in 1911 for creating a method for measuring radioactivity. She directed the study of radioactivity at the University of Paris and developed mobile x-ray units, known as *Petites Curies*, that were used in the diagnosis of injuries near the battlefields of World War I.

In 1934, after suffering from aplastic pernicious anemia, caused by radiation exposure, Marie Curie died aged sixty-six. Because of the radioactive nature of her corpse, she was buried in a coffin lined with nearly an inch of lead. In 1995, Marie and Pierre's remains were moved to the Pantheon, where France's most esteemed historical figures are laid to rest. One of her two daughters, Irene, continued her mother's work and was awarded a Nobel Prize for the discovery of artificial radiation. Curie's granddaughter was also a nuclear physicist.

Who was "the mother of the atomic bomb"?

Albert Einstein called her the "German Marie Curie" (see previous page), but unlike her French physics counterpart, she never received fame and fortune from her scientific discoveries. Despite being a committed pacifist, Lise Meitner's name is largely associated with the development of the atomic bomb.

Great Passion, Great Teachers

Born in 1878, Lise Meitner was an Austrian Jewish girl with an interest in a scientific education at a time when none of these things worked in her favor. Thanks to her parents' enthusiasm for their children's education, Meitner received private tutelage in physics and was admitted to the University of Vienna in her early twenties. Meitner became only the second woman to graduate from the university with a physics doctorate. She went on to support Stefan Meyer in his study of alpha particles and was personal assistant to Max Planck, who originated quantum theory and won the Nobel Prize in 1918.

It was while working for Planck that she met Otto Hahn, who would become her research partner for the next thirty years. Hahn was the methodical and brilliant chemist to Meitner's exceptional theorist—they were the perfect pair. Based at Berlin's Kaiser-Wilhelm Institute for Chemistry, they published a number of important papers, and the Hahn-Meitner research team was soon one of the world's most celebrated physics partnerships—they were nominated for the Nobel Prize for ten consecutive years.

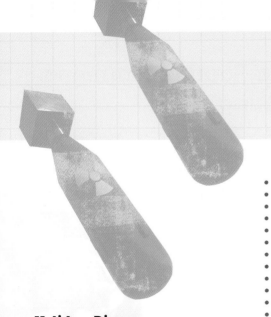

Allied scientists soon realized that this fission reaction could be used to produce an extremely powerful bomb, and they convinced President Roosevelt to fund the Manhattan Project to create it. Meitner was offered the chance to be involved but famously retorted: "I will have nothing to do with a bomb!" In 1945, the same year nuclear weapons were dropped on the Japanese cities of Hiroshima and Nagasaki, Hahn received the Nobel Prize in Chemistry for their work—Meitner never received any of the credit.

Holiday Discovery

In 1938, in the midst of their experiments, the new anti-Semitic laws of Hitler's Third Reich meant Meitner was forced to leave Germany. She fled to Sweden, where she continued their research through letters and secret meetings. Since the neutron was discovered in 1932 scientists began bombarding uranium with neutrons to see what would happen to the unstable isotope. Hahn and his research partner Fritz Strassmann's experiments established that rather than get heavier, the uranium atoms actually got lighter when smashed with neutrons. He wrote to Meitner saying: "Perhaps you can come up with some sort of fantastic explanation?"

That Christmas, Meitner realized that the uranium atom was probably splitting apart when bombarded with neutrons, like a drop of liquid separating into two smaller droplets. She used Einstein's mass into energy conversion equation ($E = MC^2$) to establish that the atoms were getting lighter as they expelled a large amount of energy; she also recognized that that energy could set off a chain reaction. She coined the term "nuclear fission" to describe the process of splitting the atom. In 1939, under Hahn's name alone, most likely because of Meitner's Jewish heritage, their findings appeared in the science journal *Nature*.

Why did Ayn Rand recommend stamp collecting?

After a fifty-year break from philately throughout adulthood, Ayn Rand, author of the hugely successful philosophical novels *The Fountainhead* and *Atlas Shrugged*, returned to the hobby with renewed fervor.

Stamp of Approval

In her 1971 essay, "Why I Like Stamp Collecting," the Russian-American Rand outlined a plethora of reasons: from using it as a cure for mental fatigue while writing to the pleasure of independent action alongside the struggles of her career. It was the perfect hobby to complement her objectivist philosophy, where productive achievements and personal happiness are the motivating pursuits of life. She chose stamps over other collectibles because, she wrote, "stamps are the concrete, visible symbols of an enormous abstraction: of the communications net embracing the world." She amassed over 50,000 stamps. In 1999, had she still been alive, Rand would have had a very special addition to her collection: The U.S. Postal Service issued a 33-cent stamp dedicated to her as part of the American Literary Arts Series.

The Collectors

The first ever postage stamp, the Penny Black, was issued in the United Kingdom in 1840 and featured an image of a young Queen Victoria. Stamp collections were started soon afterward. Ayn Rand was not the only famous woman to enjoy the pursuit of philately. Other well-known collectors include Queen Elizabeth II, who has added significantly to the Royal Philatelic Collection, thought to be the most comprehensive collection of British and Commonwealth stamps; aviator Amelia Earhart, who sold her own stamp souvenirs to fund her air travel; and tennis player Maria Sharapova.

How did a nurse change the way polio was treated?

With no formal training, Australian bush nurse Elizabeth Kenny probably didn't expect to revolutionize polio treatment. But after successfully treating children with polio in the outback, she set her sights on the world.

Against the Grain

Sister Kenny, as she was later known after earning the senior nursing title while working for the Australian Army Nursing Service in England during World War I, spent the inter-war years opening clinics in her native Australia to treat polio—what was then one of the most widespread childhood viral diseases in the world. Its symptoms include fever, aching muscles, and in some cases temporary or permanent paralysis. Her method, of using hot

towels to bandage painful limbs and then bending and flexing the joints, was widely criticized by the medical profession. The standard treatment for polio at the time was immobilization of the limbs using splints and braces. The Kenny method, as it was later known, meant the patient took an active role in their rehabilitation, and many regained movement in what were only temporarily paralyzed limbs.

Institutional Success

Despite the medical establishment's condemnation of Sister Kenny, she traveled to the United States to demonstrate her method at the Mayo Clinic and the University of Minnesota. It was there that she found national fame and in 1942 founded the Sister Kenny Institute, offering rehabilitation treatment for polio patients. The institute also offered courses so that other practitioners could learn the method. In 1955 a polio vaccine was developed, the widespread use of which dramatically reduced cases. The Americas were declared completely polio free in 1994. The institute would go on to provide more general rehabilitation medicine.

Who helped Albert Einstein with his math problems?

Mileva Marić's name might not be familiar, but she was the first wife of *Time* magazine's Person of the Twentieth Century, Albert Einstein, and a scientist in her own right. So what part did she play in the Nobel Prize winner's success?

Clever Classmates

Born in the Austro-Hungarian Empire in 1875, Marić came from a wealthy, respected family. After she'd traveled to Serbia to study, her father received special permission from the Ministry of Education so she could attend the Royal Classical Gymnasium in Zagreb and attend physics classes (typically boys-only affairs). After high school she was the only woman admitted alongside four men to the Polytechnic Institute in Zurich to study physics and mathematics. Albert Einstein was one of her classmates. They became inseparable, helping each other to study. From surviving correspondence between the pair, it is clear that the more organized Marić helped Einstein to focus on his work.

Signs of the Times

Marić and Einstein were in a relationship, but his German family were not supportive. Marić was four years his senior, an intellectual, and a "foreigner," which likely contributed to their disapproval. And Einstein didn't have a job, although at least he graduated. Despite excelling at school work and having similar grades to Einstein, when they finished their studies in 1900, Marić didn't get a high enough score and missed out on her degree. Then Marić became pregnant. In 1902, still unmarried, Marić gave birth to their daughter. It's thought the child was given up for adoption, although her fate is unclear.

In various letters to Marić during these years, Einstein often refers to his work as "our work," and it's widely believed her name was taken off certain papers she contributed to, perhaps in an effort to help further Einstein's career. In one letter he wrote: "How happy and proud will I be when the two of us together will have brought our work on relative motion to a victorious conclusion!"

Contributor or Sounding Board?

The following year, Einstein found employment and they finally got married. They would go on to have two sons. In 1905, Einstein published a number of important articles, including one on special relativity and another on the photoelectric effect. The latter would eventually earn him the 1921 Nobel Prize for Physics. Biographers of both Einstein and Marić believe that his wife was fundamental in checking these important works, writing his lecture notes, and offering her insights and opinions, while others think she was nothing more than a sounding board. According to one account, at a gathering of intellectuals at Marić's brother's house, Einstein was reported as saying: "I need my wife. She solves for me all my mathematical problems." She might not have had her name attached to any prizes, but Marić did benefit from Einstein's big win—in their 1919 divorce settlement, after he'd left her for his cousin, Elsa Lowenthal, he agreed that if he ever won the prize, she would receive the money.

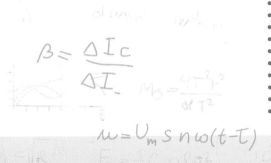

What did Pickering's computers do?

When we think of computers, we think of machines that help us with everyday tasks: laptops, mobile phones, even watches . . . but in the late nineteenth century the term was used to refer to a very important group of women.

Progressive Pickering

Edward Pickering was from New England and had graduated from Harvard in 1865. He taught physics at Massachusetts Institute of Technology (MIT), encouraging students to take part in experiments rather than just observing—revolutionary teaching for the time—and welcoming a woman, Sarah Frances Whiting, the first professor of physics at women's college Wellesley, into his classroom. He would carry this pioneering approach with him when he became the director of Harvard College Observatory in 1877. At this time, under Pickering's

directorship, a new technology was being harnessed: astrophotography. While previously astronomers had relied on telescopic observations and their notes, astrophotography attached a camera to the telescope to take photos, which could then be analyzed in greater detail and returned to time and again. In 1878, developments by Charles Bennett meant that the glass-plate photographs astronomers could take were as clear as what they could see with their own eyes.

Photographing the Stars

The only problem? There was a vast amount of photographic data that needed to be classified and analyzed. In total, 500,000 photographic plates arrived from observatories all over the world. While there were few women considered smart enough to study the stars, Pickering deemed them useful (and the cost of employing them cheap enough) to take on the tedious work of using mathematical formulae to calculate the coordinates of stars and their brightness, classifying the stars through comparison, cataloging the photographs with notes, and transferring all that information into tables.

Over his forty-two-year tenure, more than eighty women worked under Pickering, many putting in six-day weeks for very low pay. Initially he hired female relatives and maids, then women with office experience and math skills were recruited. As more colleges began to accept women, the skill level of the Harvard computers, as they came to be known, increased. Most women weren't allowed to make telescopic observations, but their work made an important contribution to wider astronomical theory.

Stellar Effort

Some of the female computers were not content just being part of "Pickering's harem" and went on to make names for themselves.

ANNIE JUMP CANNON was a Wellesley College graduate who studied under Whiting. She simplified an existing stellar cataloging system, which was adopted by the International Astronomical Union. Known as the Harvard spectral classification system, it is still used today.

WILLIAMINA FLEMING was Pickering's maid before he employed her as a full-time copyist and Harvard computer. She worked at Harvard for thirty-four years, managing the computer staff, and was appointed curator of astronomical photos in 1899.

HENRIETTA SWAN LEAVITT was a Harvard graduate who was hired to measure and catalog the brightness of certain stars between exposures. She came up with a way for astronomers to measure distance in space from the images, known as Leavitt's Law.

QUESTION 39

What did scientists see for the first time in Photo 51?

Photo 51 is no ordinary photograph—it was the final clue needed to determine the structure of DNA following decades of research. It is considered one of the most important images ever taken.

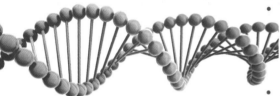

Taking Shape

Taken in May 1952 at King's College in London, by biophysicist Rosalind Franklin and her PhD student Raymond Gosling, the photo is of a tiny sample of hydrated DNA. The DNA sample would have been fixed to a support and sealed in a camera. In a process called X-ray crystallography, it then had an X-ray beam shone at it for more than sixty hours. The X-rays would bounce off the molecule's atoms and the pattern created on film helped scientists to determine the molecule's structure. In Photo 51, the darker areas represent the four parts of DNA which make up our genetic code, and the cross pattern of spots represent the planes of symmetry of the double-helix shape.

Race to Discovery

Franklin and Gosling, as well as Maurice Wilkins, at King's College were in a three-way race with James Watson and Frances Crick at Cambridge University and Linus Pauling at the California Institute of Technology to figure out the structure of DNA. Keen to make progress and beat the American, Wilkins showed Franklin's photograph to Watson. It was enough to help Watson and Crick figure out the double helix. It was one of the most important scientific discoveries of all time, for which Watson, Crick, and Wilkins shared the Nobel Prize in 1962. No mention was made of Franklin, who had died in 1958 of ovarian cancer. The prize cannot be received posthumously.

Why was Margaret Cavendish's visit to the Royal Society so controversial?

In May 1667, the Duchess of Newcastle, Margaret Cavendish, attended a meeting of the Royal Society, arguably the world's most important scientific establishment. The existing fellows were up in arms—protesting her presence. Why? Because she was a woman.

Girls not Allowed

Women were not permitted to become members of the society until 1945, 285 years after the society was founded. Other than Queen Victoria becoming a patron in 1838, the first official female fellows were crystallographer Kathleen Lonsdale and biochemist Marjory Stephenson. And the society wasn't alone in its rejection of women members. The American National Academy of Sciences didn't allow women members until 1925 and France's Académie des Sciences waited until 1962 to let women through its doors.

An Interest in Science

Cavendish was married to William Cavendish, a wealthy aristocrat who socialized with the leading philosophers, playwrights, and poets of the day. He was more than happy to discuss scientific advances and philosophy with his wife. Margaret knew many of the Royal Society's most prominent fellows, and this was no doubt how she gained entry to the inner sanctum, however scandalous it may have been. During her visit she watched experiments being conducted—Samuel Pepys described her as being "full of admiration"—but she later attacked the society for its stale approach, use of vivisection, and ban on women. Margaret Cavendish was a prolific writer, publishing numerous poems, plays, and what many consider to be one of the first works of science fiction: *A Description of a New World Called the Blazing World*, in which a woman becomes the ruler of a utopian realm.

Why was Hypatia beaten to death?

QUESTION 41 QUESTION

While she went on to become a mere footnote in the lives of the men who fought around her, Hypatia was so much more: A pioneering woman of her time whose scholarly skills drew crowds and ultimately led to her downfall.

Who was Hypatia?

What is known about Hypatia largely comes from writings about other people. But it is widely understood that her father was the mathematician Theon and she was born around AD 350 (although this is disputed); her mother is unknown. Theon taught her all he knew, and it's thought she collaborated with him on—or even wrote—some of his important works. She progressed to become a math and science teacher in her own right, as well as a philosopher. She was a member of the Neoplatonic school of philosophy and, like male intellectuals, she would wear academic robes and give popular public lectures on the teachings of Plato and Aristotle. While she never married, she was described as being "exceedingly beautiful," and was afforded a "special respect" by the people of Alexandria.

Religious War

During the fourth century, the Roman Empire saw the growth of Christianity where once paganism had been the status quo. In Alexandria, a cultural center in the ancient world, pagans, Jews, and Christians rubbed alongside each other. Civil war soon followed, and the city was overrun by fighting between the various religious groups. During Hypatia's time in Alexandria, there was a political struggle between the head of the government, Orestes, who was protective of the city's Jewish community, and the head of the Christian church, Cyril. They were locked in a feud over ecclesiastical reform, which resulted in a massacre of Christians by the Jewish people, who were angry after being provoked by the Christians at a public hearing. Cyril then led a crowd through the city to kick out the Jews, looting their temples and homes in the process. Cyril even tried to have Orestes assassinated, despite his attempts at reconciliation.

The Perfect Scapegoat

As a pagan woman who preached to the masses about non-Christian philosophy, Hypatia was a public nuisance to the Christians, and the perfect scapegoat for their cause. She was also an easier target—Orestes, wary after the assassination attempt on him, was usually surrounded by armed guards. It's not clear how much of a role Cyril played in Hypatia's murder, but soon a rumor began to spread around the city that Hypatia, whom Orestes admired, was preventing the warring leaders from reconciliation. She had to be killed.

Murdered by the Mob

Hypatia was traveling through the city in AD 415 when a Christian zealot mob led by a man named Peter the Lector surrounded her carriage and dragged her from it into a nearby church. She was stripped and beaten to death with either roofing tiles or oyster shells. Those same weapons were then used to tear her to pieces. Her body might also have been dragged through the streets. When they were done, the mob burned her remains.

What did Marie Tharp chart on sheets of white linen?

Marie Tharp started life as the daughter of a soil surveyor and ended it as one of the world's greatest cartographers. Her work dramatically changed how we see our planet both above and below the ocean's surface.

Rocky Start

She may have enjoyed collecting soil samples with her father, but coming of age in the late 1930s, Tharp would never have expected to pursue a career in the earth sciences. Working in those fields just wasn't an option for most women. She graduated from Ohio University in 1943, having majored in English and music. But the world had other plans. After America entered World War II, there was a serious shortage of professionals in the male-dominated areas of science and technology. To combat the problem, women were soon being encouraged to pursue degrees in the sciences.

Tharp jumped at the chance and enrolled in an accelerated geology course at the University of Michigan. Her mentor encouraged her to take a course in drafting, knowing it would be an employable skill she could use to work in the industry (field work was

still off-limits to women). The effort paid off. In 1948 she found a job at the prestigious Lamont Geological Observatory at Columbia University, where cutting-edge research was the order of the day.

An Ocean of Possibility

The observatory was engaged in a huge undertaking—mapping the ocean floor. Before the development of sonar technology during World War II, the ocean floor had largely been regarded as flat. Now it was possible for ships to determine the precise depth of the earth below them. Years of data had been amassed and it was Tharp's job to check through it all and plot the findings onto a huge map made from linen fabric. Because the lab's director considered women "bad luck" on these research trips, Tharp didn't join a research vessel for fifteen years.

The resulting 5,000-foot linen scroll was a collaboration between Tharp and geologist Bruce Charles Heezen, who obtained the data. The results were astonishing. Tharp's maps revealed mountains, canyons, and ridges as spectacular as those seen above sea level. Most surprisingly, her drawings illustrated a 10,000-mile underwater mountain range and rift valley that ran down the middle of the Atlantic Ocean, which they later discovered was part of a much larger mid-ocean ridge system. This was evidence that at some point magma had emerged from inside the earth, forming a new crust and forcing the continents apart. She had found the largest geographical feature on the planet and evidence to support the theories of sea-spreading and continental drift.

Acceptance and Recognition

Heezen made some of their findings public in 1957 and shook the geological world to its core with new theories emerging about how the planet and the living organisms on its surface evolved. Despite shying away from the spotlight, Tharp continued to work alongside Heezen until he died in 1977. But in 1997, she was suitably honored for her field-changing work with a double honors from the Library of Congress. It named her one of the four greatest cartographers of the twentieth century—those drafting skills came in useful after all.

Who was the first woman to earn a university degree?

In 1672, Gianbattista Cornaro Piscopia, a prominent Venetian nobleman, bought a house for his daughter Elena near the University of Padua so she could study there. She would become the school's first female graduate, an achievement unheard of at the time in Europe.

Graduating Sexism

Despite Elena's gender, her father ensured she received an extensive education, just like her brothers. Born in 1646, by the time Elena went to university, she was already fluent in seven languages. She had been tutored in math, astronomy, philosophy, music, and theology. And it was in theology that she hoped to earn a degree. The Roman Catholic Church wouldn't permit it, but she was allowed to pursue a philosophy degree instead. On June 25, 1678, her degree defense was held at the city's Cathedral of the Blessed Virgin to accommodate all the spectators. The thirty-two-year-old became the first woman to earn a doctorate degree from a university.

Her True Calling

Despite her academic achievements, what Elena wanted most of all was to be a Benedictine nun. She had secretly taken a vow of chastity aged eleven, much to her father's chagrin. He hoped to marry her off to another influential family, but she turned down a number of proposals, choosing instead to become an oblate (lay nun) of the Benedictine order. She wore the order's habit underneath her expensive dresses. Elena continued to do charitable work until her death and was buried, at her request, in a small chapel in Padua's Basilica of Santa Giustina, rather than in the extravagant family tomb.

THINKERS

They might be smarter than you, but that doesn't mean you can't remember some thought-provoking details about these academic powerhouses.
Ace this test, smarty-pants!

Questions

1. What year was a polio vaccine created?

2. Who did Samuel Pepys describe as being "full of admiration" during her visit to the Royal Society?

3. Which important female scientist turned down the chance to work on the Manhattan Project?

4. What is the chemical element polonium named after?

5. What did university graduate Elena Cornaro Piscopia really want to do with her life?

6. What was the first postage stamp called?

7. What philosophical school did Hypatia belong to?

8. Why wasn't cartographer Marie Tharp allowed on research vessels for fifteen years?

9. Who created the Harvard spectral classification system?

10. Who won the 1921 Nobel Prize for Physics?

Turn to page 214 for the answers.

WHY DID ELEANOR OF AQUITAINE MARRY TWO RIVAL KINGS?

WHY WOULDN'T YOU WANT TO SPEND THE NIGHT WITH AMINA?

HOW MANY ASSASSINATION ATTEMPTS DID QUEEN VICTORIA SURVIVE?

WHO WAS HATSHEPSUT AND WHY DID SHE WEAR A FAKE BEARD?

LEADERS

WHAT MADE CATHERINE THE GREAT SO GREAT?

WHY WAS AUNG SAN SUU KYI PLACED UNDER HOUSE ARREST?

Who was Hatshepsut and why did she wear a fake beard?

After her pharaoh husband, Thutmose II, died in 1479 BC, Hatshepsut became his young son's coregent. It wasn't unusual—widowed queens often took on the role—but then she did something unprecedented, declaring herself pharaoh and coruler.

Wicked Stepmother?

Hatshepsut wasn't the first female pharaoh, but she was the first to assume power while there was a living male heir. The young king, Thutmose III, wasn't Hatshepsut's son, but the offspring of another wife in her husband's harem. She wasn't shy about her self-appointed position—she had impressive architectural structures built in her honor, such as her own mortuary temple. While it would be easy to assume that Hatshepsut was seizing power from her stepson, it's more likely she projected an image of strength to secure the throne for his future.

Either way, her fifteen-year reign was a peaceful one with notable advances in art and culture. She made sure her stepson received the best education available, the kind normally only accessible to scribes and priests, and he also went off to join the military, preparing him for the demands of his future. When he was ready to rule, she handed over the throne without a fight, declaring Thutmose III the supreme commander of the military. And all her efforts paid off. Thutmose III became one of ancient Egypt's great pharaohs.

For a long time Hatshepsut's impact on Egyptian life was unknown—after her death, Thutmose III erased most of the depictions of her, tearing down statues and scratching her name out of records. Only recent archaeological discoveries have helped to reinstate her to her rightful position in history as one of the most significant female rulers of the period.

Bearded Lady

Early depictions of Hatshepsut show her as a woman, such as on some blocks archaeologists discovered on Elephantine Island in Egypt. But in her later years a more muscular, masculine image emerged, and Hatshepsut started to be represented as a male king—probably at her own request to maintain a strong and powerful image. One typical garment for Egyptian pharaohs was a false metallic beard, which they wore over a clean-shaven face. It's believed this was in an effort to be associated with the god Osiris, who was also depicted to have a grand synthetic beard of his own. These beards were coveted possessions, often passed down between rulers.

MUMMY MYSTERY

In 1902 Howard Carter discovered Hatshepsut's tomb in the Valley of the Kings, but when her sarcophagus was opened eighteen years later it was found to be empty. Then, in 2007, archaeologists decided to reinvestigate and examined two other sarcophagi found in a nonroyal tomb. One of them had an inscription identifying the mummy as Hatshepsut's wet nurse. The other was removed and taken to Cairo where it underwent a CT scan. The scan revealed the mummified remains of a forty-five- to sixty-year-old woman with missing teeth. Hatshepsut's original tomb was filled with artifacts belonging to the ruler, including a box containing a tooth. Experts were able to match that tooth to the unknown mummy—Hatshepsut's body had finally been found.

Which French queen was an unintentional porn star?

Marie Antoinette married Louis XVI of France in 1770, becoming Queen of France and Navarre when he ascended to the throne four years later. But the royal family's extravagant spending, as well as poor political and economic decisions, meant there was growing dissent among the people. And public popularity for the queen soon waned . . .

Married Mistress

With revolution on the horizon, political propaganda against the royal family swelled. In the past, the popular *libelles*—smutty political pamphlets—had taken aim at a monarch's mistresses. But Louis XVI had none, so it was Marie Antoinette who took the brunt of the tabloids' gossip.

LET THEM EAT LIES

When people think of Marie Antoinette they think of her famous retort "Let them eat cake!" in response to being told the French people had no bread to eat, but it's unlikely she ever said it. This phrase had been attributed to foreign queens marrying into the French royal family for decades. It was a way of venting the public's frustration at the growing economic inequality, taking it out on a foreigner rather than their own king. That's not to say the royals didn't live extravagant lives—the queen wore white flour in her wigs to follow fashion while the French people had no bread to eat. The king's brother was even said to order a new pair of shoes for every day of the year.

The pamphlets included cartoons that depicted the queen in all manner of pornographic situations. From orgies to lesbianism and incest, she was shown always with an insatiable appetite for sex, cavorting with her brother-in-law, servants, or even her own children. Her husband was usually depicted as disinterested or impotent. This, at least, was based in truth. The royal couple, who were married as teenagers, took seven years to produce an heir to the throne. There were reports that the king had a painful medical condition that caused impotency. There is little actual evidence that Marie Antoinette had sexual relationships with other men, but that didn't stop the rumor mill from painting her as an immoral woman.

Ridiculed to Death

The *libelles* were powerful, especially considering that at the time there was no official royal press office to counteract the lies they spread. The pamphlets were even sold outside the gates of the Tuileries Palace, the royal family's Paris residence. While perhaps 10 percent of the publications ridiculed the queen prior to 1789, once the French Revolution began, the majority took aim at her. While the *libelles* did not themselves incite revolution, they encouraged the opinion that the monarchy was corrupt and the king was incompetent.

In August 1792, a group of revolutionary radicals invaded the Tuileries Palace and arrested Louis. A month later the monarchy was abolished and, after standing trial, the king was sent to the guillotine. Marie Antoinette followed nine months later. By the time she was executed in 1793, public perception of her was of a frivolous and immoral woman.

How many assassination attempts did Queen Victoria survive?

Until very recently, Queen Victoria was the United Kingdom's longest-ruling monarch, but her lengthy reign, and life, was almost cut short a staggering eight times.

Marital Woes

On June 10, 1840, four months after Queen Victoria and Prince Albert celebrated their wedding, an attempt was made on the monarch's life. The newlyweds were leaving Buckingham Palace in an open-top carriage when eighteen-year-old barman Edward Oxford stepped from the crowd and fired two pistols at the queen. The first shot missed as the queen turned to look at a horse, and she managed to duck the second shot. The crowd descended on the assassin as the carriage continued on its journey. The couple still took their turn around the park to show the public the queen hadn't been harmed. Oxford was found guilty by reason of insanity and spent twenty-four years in a mental asylum before being deported to Australia.

Caught in the Act

The royal couple hadn't learned their lesson. Two years later they were leaving a Sunday church service at St. James's Palace, again in an open-top carriage, when another would-be assassin pointed a pistol at the queen and pulled the trigger. Luckily, the gun failed to fire, but the man wielding it, a carpenter called John Francis, made his escape into the crowd. Rather than be confined to the palace, fearing for her life, the queen made the decision to head out the very next day to entice the would-be assassin to return. This time in a closed carriage, the couple made their usual journey through the

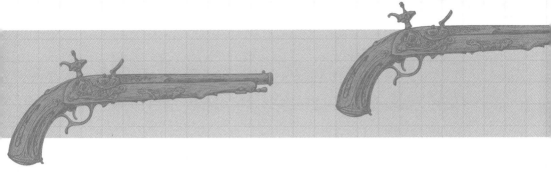

city's parks, but plain-clothes police officers were on the lookout for anyone matching the description Prince Albert had provided. The temptation proved too much for Francis and he fired at the couple again. When a shot rang out, a police officer spotted the shooter and he was arrested immediately.

Insane Assassins

Oxford and Francis were both found to be legally insane for their attempt to kill the queen, and sentenced accordingly, and over the next thirty years three more men would face the same fate. They included a disabled teenager, a disgruntled Irishman, and a clerk who made it a foot away from the queen before being wrestled off her by her trusted servant John Brown. The only would-be assassin found to be of sound mind by a jury was Robert Pate. In 1850 the former army officer struck Victoria across the head with a cane, causing bruising to her face. Luckily, her bonnet absorbed most of the impact.

The Final Attempt

The queen was a grieving widow and sixty-three years old in 1882 when she faced the final threat to her life. She had arrived at Windsor station by train and was traveling to the castle in her carriage. The monarch was shocked by a noise she assumed to be an engine explosion, but it was actually the sound of twenty-eight-year-old Roderick Maclean trying to shoot her. The man was beaten by two umbrella-wielding school boys from nearby Eton, who happened to be at the train station. This final attempt helped to secure the queen's popularity at a time when it was waning. She later said of the incident, "It is worth being shot at to see how much one is loved."

Why was Aung San Suu Kyi placed under house arrest?

A ung San Suu Kyi was born in Myanmar (or Burma, as it is still called by some countries) in 1945. The country is a melting pot of 135 officially recognized ethnicities. Her father, Aung San, was a general who tried to end colonial British rule by uniting the various groups for a common cause. But despite being regarded as the founder of the modern nation of Myanmar, six months before independence was achieved in 1948, he was assassinated. Suu Kyi was just two years old.

A Life Abroad

Over a decade of tribal conflicts followed. In 1960, Suu Kyi's mother, Daw Khin Kyi, was appointed ambassador to India, so she moved to Delhi with her teenage daughter. Later, while Suu Kyi studied at Oxford University in England in the early 1960s, in Burma the military seized power, changing the country's name to Myanmar and embarking on a repressive regime that would last for half a century. Suu Kyi finally returned to her homeland in 1988 to nurse her sick mother. In the intervening years, she'd married and raised two children with her British husband. She was greeted by a country riddled with poverty and a growing appetite for democracy.

Daughter of a Hero

That year, people took to the streets in protest against military leader General Ne Win. Suu Kyi witnessed the regime's brutality as soldiers fired on the crowds, killing hundreds. She was her father's daughter, and when she was asked to lead a new political party, the National League for Democracy (NLD), she accepted despite having no political experience. Her family name held a lot of weight and she became the figurehead of a nonviolent campaign for peaceful democracy.

A Prisoner in Her Own Home

The junta, the military-run government, announced there would be general elections in 1990. It seemed the public pressure had worked. But it wasn't to be. Suu Kyi was placed under house arrest, as was the majority of her party's leadership. They still won the election by a huge majority, but the military refused to release its grip on the country. Over the next twenty-one years, Suu Kyi would spend fifteen of them under house arrest in her own home in Yangon. She remained loyal to her democratic mission, even when her husband, still in England, received a terminal cancer diagnosis. She never saw him before he died. In 2011, she was finally released.

A New Government

In 1991 she received the Nobel Peace Prize for her leadership of the pro-democracy movement. And in 2015, when Myanmar was allowed free elections for the first time in twenty-five years, her popularity saw that the NLD won by a mile. Suu Kyi was barred from running for president because of her non-Burmese children; instead she received the title "state counselor." The military agreed to share power with the party and formed a new government. However, in the years since, the government, including Suu Kyi, have been criticized internationally for the military's treatment of the Rohingya minority. The Rohingya have faced shocking ethnic violence, forcing them to flee the country in their thousands.

Who was the "Joan of Arc of Africa"?

An inspirational figure from Ghanaian history, Yaa Asantewaa was a warrior queen who stood up to the colonial British when the men around her were ready to give in.

The Golden Stool

In the late 1800s, the gold-mining Asante nation (in modern-day Ghana) had been forcibly taken over by British rule. By 1900, the invaders had exiled most of the local leaders, including Yaa Asantewaa's grandson, King Prempeh I. The nation's most sacred possession was the Golden Stool (an immense golden throne), and British Colonial Secretary Sir Frederick Mitchell Hodgson wanted it. He knew that ownership of the stool would be symbolic of the colonial power's dominance over the locals.

A Rousing Speech

The remaining chiefs held a meeting to decide what to do, but it was Yaa Asantewaa who inspired them to fight. "Is it true that the bravery of the Asante is no more?" she asked them in a rousing speech. "If you, the men of Asante, will not go forward, then we will. I shall call upon my fellow women . . . We will fight till the last of us falls on the battlefield!"

Her speech did the trick—she was elected to lead the army, making her the first and only woman to do so. Starting in April 1900, she commanded a three-month siege of a British garrison, known as the War of the Golden Stool. While the British ultimately defeated the Asante people, arresting Yaa Asantewaa in 1901 and exiling her to the Seychelles, she remains a Ghanaian cultural symbol of defiance, bravery, and female power— the "Joan of Arc of Africa."

"I shall call upon my fellow women . . . We will fight till the last of us falls on the battlefield!"

Which ancient ruler was a founding member of the Inimitable Livers society?

Renowned for her power, intelligence, and beauty, Egyptian ruler Cleopatra was one of Ancient Egypt's most important political players (her reign was also the last of the 300-year-old Ptolemaic dynasty). But she also knew how to have fun.

Living Life to the Full

The Inimitable Livers society (referring to life rather than the internal organ) was founded by Cleopatra and her Roman lover Marc Antony in 41 BC. The group was said to be dedicated to Dionysus, the Greek god of winemaking, fertility, and ritual madness—a feasting club for merry-making, debauchery, and pranks. Later, when Roman ruler Octavian was preparing to invade Egypt, the pair started a new society to eat and drink the days away in light of their impending doom. It was known as The Companions in Death.

Queen With a Pearl Earring

At one gathering of the Inimitable Livers, it's reported that Cleopatra made a bet with Antony that she could spend 10,000,000 sestertii, the ancient Roman coin, on their next lavish dinner. It was a huge amount of money,

estimated to be millions of dollars in modern currency.

Antony took the bet. At their next dinner he watched in confusion as an ordinary feast was presented before him. For the second course a servant brought a cup of vinegar and placed it in front of Cleopatra. She took out one of her priceless pearl earrings and dropped it into the cup. After the pearl had dissolved, she lifted the goblet and drank its contents. One of the most expensive meals of all time.

Why did Eleanor of Aquitaine marry two rival kings?

On May 18, 1152, at Poitiers Cathedral in France, Eleanor of Aquitaine married Henry Plantagenet, Count of Anjou and Duke of Normandy. She was eleven years older than her nineteen-year-old groom, but that wasn't the only notable thing about her. On the contrary. Only two months before she had been married to another man: King Louis VII of France.

A Marriage of Inheritance

Eleanor was the oldest daughter of William X, Duke of Aquitaine. Her father owned more of France than the king, and she was well-educated and highly cultured. She would have been an eligible young woman regardless; however, in 1137, her father and only brother died, leaving her with a vast inheritance. Her matrimonial prospects shot through the roof, and at fifteen she was married to King Louis IV of France's son. He became King Louis VII shortly after. The couple had two daughters, but their union failed to produce a son—a sticking point in their marriage that likely drove a wedge between the couple.

She was an adventurous queen, and despite their marital problems she was keen to travel with her husband. She accompanied him to Constantinople and Jerusalem on the doomed Second Crusade in 1147—when Louis and Germany's Conrad III led a European military force to try and retake the Holy Land. They were badly beaten by the Seljuk Turks. In March 1152, after she had been the Queen of France for fifteen years, the marriage was annulled on the grounds of consanguinity—that they were descended from the same bloodline—and Eleanor's lands returned to her private ownership.

My Husband, My King

Within two years of Eleanor marrying Henry, he was crowned Henry II of England at Westminster Cathedral. Their union had brought together her inherited lands in the southwest of

France with his Angevin territories in Britain and northern France to create a vast empire. The couple had eight children, although one died young, including five of the sons Louis had longed for. Three of those boys would go on to become kings of England: Henry the Young King, Richard I, and John. For two decades the couple traveled their domain to make sure the cross-cultural monarchy was seen to

be present by the people. Eleanor spent lots of time with her children, brokering powerful marriages for them, and played a prominent part in government, particularly when Henry was away.

Motherly Devotion

Sadly, Eleanor's second marriage was headed in the same direction as her first. Eleanor and Henry's stormy relationship, acerbated by his multiple affairs, effectively came to an end in 1173. She sided with her sons, Richard and John, when they rebelled against their father. After the rebellion failed, Henry had Eleanor placed under house arrest, and she was shut away for the next fifteen years until his death in 1189. In later life, she was involved in the reigns of both sons. By the time she died in 1204, she had spent nearly seventy years being one of the most powerful women in Europe.

Who was the Bisley Boy?

She was the famous "Virgin Queen" who never married and ruled England for forty-five years, but Elizabeth I's decision to remain single when the monarchy had always sought advantageous unions, both for political reasons and to produce heirs, meant there was never a short supply of rumors about her. Including one that the queen wasn't a queen at all, but a king in disguise . . .

Switched as a Child

Elizabeth was never supposed to be queen. She was the child of Henry VIII and his second wife, Anne Boleyn. Her father had her mother beheaded for adultery and treason when Elizabeth was just three years old, and as a result she spent most of her childhood raised in a separate household to the royal family. The local legend goes that in 1542, when the future queen was

nine, Henry VIII left his daughter at a royal hunting lodge in Bisley, Surrey, to protect her from the plague while he joined the Berkeley Hunt in Gloucestershire. According to the tale, Elizabeth died while her father was gone, but the courtiers, fearful of the repercussions for not protecting the princess, devised a plan to save themselves. They found a local redheaded boy who closely resembled Elizabeth, dressed him as the princess, and carried on as if nothing had happened. The Bisley Boy would go on to become the Queen of England.

"Womanish Infirmity"

Conspiracy theorists have suggested exhuming Elizabeth's body to check that she was actually a woman. But it's highly unlikely that the Bisley Boy story is true. For starters, Elizabeth may not have married, but she did have intimate relationships with male courtiers, most notably with Robert Dudley, the Earl of Leicester. She also had close relationships with her ladies-in-waiting—if she'd actually been a man, it would have been hard to keep it a secret for long. That said, there were more serious suspicions that Elizabeth refused to marry

DRESSED TO IMPRESS

She might not have been in the market for a husband, but that didn't stop Elizabeth from taking pride in her appearance. It took her ladies-in-waiting four hours to dress and undress the queen each day. She wore her iconic red-headed wigs as well as a considerable amount of makeup, especially as she got older to maintain the appearance of youth. This pale "mask" was made from white lead and vinegar and was painted on to her face, neck, and hands. This mixture, known as ceruse, was actually speeding up the ageing process, corroding the queen's skin. She also wore black kohl eyeliner and red lipstick made from beeswax and plant dye.

because she had a "womanish infirmity," a medical condition that would prevent her from having a baby. The rumor persisted to the point that a foreign ambassador bribed the queen's servants to report on the state of her bedsheets—they were trying to determine if she was menstruating regularly.

Which Supreme Court Justice shares a nickname with a famous hip-hop artist?

In 1993, American President Bill Clinton made his first appointment to the Supreme Court, and in doing so appointed the second woman ever to the lifetime post of Associate Justice. The judge he chose was the U.S. Court of Appeals' indomitable Ruth Bader Ginsburg.

Top of her Class

Despite graduating from Columbia Law School at the top of her class in 1959, Ginsburg struggled to find a job after university. Most law firms at the time weren't open to women and none of the federal judges wanted a woman to clerk for them. Unlike many of her female peers, Ginsburg finally found a job with a low-ranking district court judge where she worked to prove herself for two years before moving into academia. In 1972 she set up the Women's Rights Project at the American Civil Liberties Union and became its chief counsel, participating in hundreds of gender discrimination lawsuits. She chose winnable cases that would slowly have an impact on unfair legal barriers preventing equal rights for women. She also took on some cases that showed discrimination against men. In a conservative-dominated Supreme Court, Ginsburg's dissenting speeches have become the leading voice of liberalism from the nation's highest judiciary.

Notorious Dissents

In 2013, a popular internet meme emerged referring to Ginsburg as the "Notorious RBG," a reference to rap legend Notorious BIG, also known as Biggie Smalls. It was first coined by a blog of that same name started by a New York University law graduate. The viral image of Ginsburg, wearing a crown in the same style as an infamous 1997 *Rolling Stone* cover of Biggie Smalls, combined with quotes from her dissents, helped to attract a whole new generation of people to the justice and her work. When Ginsburg first heard the nickname, she had to ask her law clerks what it was all about. In a 2015 talk at Duke University School of Law, she told the audience that she was surprised to learn her new namesake was born and raised in Brooklyn just like her.

FOLLOWING IN HER FOOTSTEPS

Ginsburg may be the longest-serving woman on the Supreme Court bench, but she was not the first. That honor went to her colleague and friend Sandra Day O'Connor, who was appointed by Ronald Reagan in 1981. For nearly twenty-five years, O'Connor was a key swing vote in a divided court on a number of important issues, including abortion and race discrimination. Despite their differing views on a number of issues, Ginsburg and O'Connor publicly praised each other on many occasions, and O'Connor regularly took on clerks who had worked with Ginsburg in federal court. The two justices served for twelve years together and were gifted matching novelty T-shirts to help identify them to anyone confused by the sight of two women on the bench. O'Connor retired in 2006, leaving Ginsburg as the lone female voice until the appointment of Sonia Sotomayor in 2009. Ginsburg has described those years as "the worst times."

What made Catherine the Great so great?

QUESTION 53

She was Russia's longest-ruling empress and one of the country's greatest leaders, but she wasn't even Russian, and her name wasn't Catherine . . . So what made her so great?

Impoverished Royalty

Born Sophie Friederike Auguste von Anhalt-Zerbst in 1729 in Prussia, now Poland, Catherine was German royalty—her father was a minor prince with little wealth and her mother a well-connected aristocrat. It was because of her mother's connections and ambitions for her children that Sophie was invited to Russia to meet Empress Elizabeth. Unmarried and childless, Elizabeth had appointed her nephew, Grand Duke Peter, as heir to the Russian throne, and she thought Sophie might be a good match for the future emperor. Sophie impressed the Russian ruler and she soon converted to the Orthodox Church, receiving her new name, Catherine. The pair were married on August 21, 1745.

Marriage and the Military

Catherine and Peter's marriage was not a happy one. It took eight years for Catherine to conceive a child, and when she did give birth, the Russian court whispered that the father wasn't Peter but a Russian military officer called Sergei Saltykov. There is even more doubt among historians as to the paternity of the three children who followed. In 1762, after Elizabeth's death, Peter III ascended to the throne, but he wasn't there for long. After he ended Russia's longstanding war with Prussia—an unpopular decision among

GREAT DEATH?

When the empress died, her enemies spread vicious rumors about her death— that when it happened she'd been on the toilet or that she'd been having sex . . . with a horse! But despite her "greatness" in life, Catherine's death was more mundane: She suffered a stroke and died in bed the following day.

the military—and proposed reforms that alienated the lower nobility, a coup ensued, forcing him to abdicate. He died shortly thereafter under suspicious circumstances. Catherine made her move, having secured the support of the nation's most powerful military leaders, and was declared empress. Her reign would last for thirty-four years.

Making Russia Great Again

The Russia she took over was bankrupted by the Seven Years' War, an international conflict that had raged across Europe and the colonies. The cost of grain was on the up, and the government was as corrupt as ever, not to mention incompetent. Catherine II (or Catherine the Great, as she would be known) regarded herself as the spiritual granddaughter of Peter the Great—her dead husband's actual grandfather—and set about continuing his policies of expansion and the spread of Western culture. The Russian empire grew considerably under her command.

Despite beginning her reign intent on social and political reform, she wasn't able to make any considerable change and relied heavily on the nobility to control the country's serf class—there were dozens of uprisings while she was on the throne. But where she really excelled herself was through her love of literature, philosophy, and art—her own collection contained 4,000 works by the likes of Raphael and Rembrandt. She transformed St. Petersburg into a center for European artists and thinkers, putting Russia on the cultural map.

Why wouldn't you want to spend the night with Amina?

She was a courageous and powerful African ruler who led the Zazzau people for thirty-four years, but most men hoped they didn't end up in her bedroom.

Preparing for Battle

Amina came from Zazzau, a province in modern-day Nigeria. She was born around 1533; her mother was the Zazzau ruler Turunku Bakwa. Her family made their money by importing metals, cloth, horses, kola nuts, and salt to the region. Other relatives, including

Amina's uncle, Karama, ascended to the throne on her mother's death. He ruled for ten years and, in the meantime, Amina trained with the best warriors to become a fearless fighter and cavalry leader. When Karama died, she'd earned so much respect from the military it was a given that she would become queen in his place.

As Capable as a Man

Over her thirty-four-year reign Amina led the 20,000-strong Zazzau military into conflict time and again, helping to expand their territory to improve trade links and maintain their regional dominance. While it might have been advantageous to do so, Zazzau never married, preferring to rule alone. However, that didn't mean she always slept alone. After every military conquest, it's said she would take a new husband—a prisoner from the defeated side, or even one of her own bodyguards—and spend the night with him. The next day the man would be executed so he could not speak of his time with the queen. In Nigeria, Amina represents the power of womanhood, and she is referred to as "woman as capable as a man."

LEADERS

Seeing as you're not running a country you don't need to worry about potential assassins, usurping family members, or putting flour in your wig. Just this quiz. On your monarch, get set . . . Go!

Questions

1. Why is Aung San Suu Kyi the state counselor of Myanmar, rather than the president?
2. What weapon did Robert Pate use to harm Queen Victoria?
3. How many years did Amina rule for?
4. What did Egyptian pharaohs wear to associate themselves with the god Osiris?
5. How is Sophie Friederike Auguste von Anhalt-Zerbst better known?
6. What did Cleopatra swallow during an Imitable Livers dinner to win a bet with Marc Antony?
7. What were the French *libelles*?
8. What did Eleanor of Aquitaine not give her French husband?
9. What did Ghanian leader Yaa Asantewaa refuse to give to the British colonialists?
10. What was the name of the mixture Queen Elizabeth I painted on her face and hands?

Turn to page 214 for the answers.

WHICH RELIGIOUS LEADER WAS KNOWN AS THE DANCING GODDESS?

WHAT'S SO SPECIAL ABOUT MOTHER TERESA'S HABIT?

WHY WAS JOAN OF ARC BURNED AT THE STAKE?

WHO IS THE ONLY AUSTRALIAN TO BE RECOGNIZED AS A SAINT BY THE CATHOLIC CHURCH?

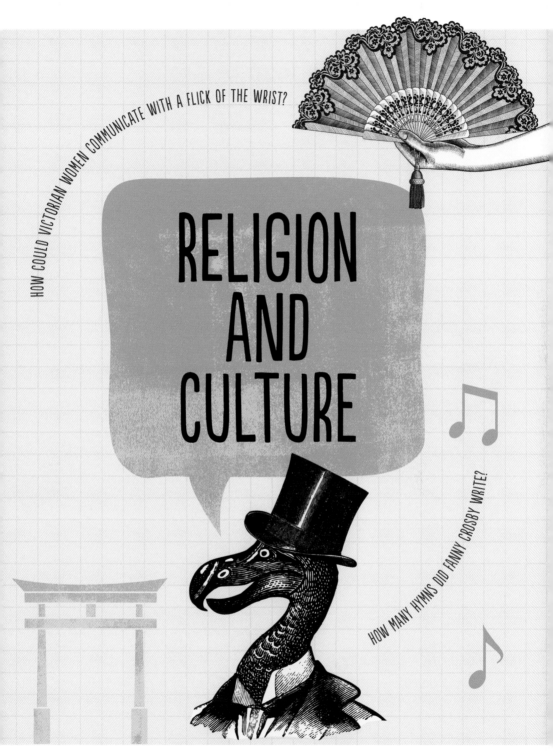

HOW COULD VICTORIAN WOMEN COMMUNICATE WITH A FLICK OF THE WRIST?

RELIGION AND CULTURE

HOW MANY HYMNS DID FANNY CROSBY WRITE?

Why was Joan of Arc burned at the stake?

FARM GIRL TURNED FASHION ICON

As well as having a penchant for menswear, Joan also lopped off her l ocks after the voices in her head told her to. The pageboy style she was known for was common among knights of the time. The English guards shaved her head before her execution, but the iconic look showed up once again many years later. In 1909, Monsieur Antoine, a popular Polish hairdresser in Paris, was inspired by Joan's look and started offering the city's fashion-forward this new short style. The bob really caught on in the 1920s and is still popular today.

Many people believe that Joan of Arc was killed because the English thought she was a witch. But the famous French military leader's execution actually had more to do with what she wore and the voices in her head.

From Cattle to Battle

One of the most revered figures from French medieval history, Joan of Arc was not a powerful monarch or esteemed intellectual but the daughter of a tenant farmer from the small village of Domrémy in northeast France. (The "Arc" was her father's surname not the place she came from, and her first name was actually Jehanne.) From 1425, when she was thirteen, Joan started hearing saints' voices and seeing visions. The voices told her to seek an audience with Charles of Valois, King Charles VI's son and, according to many, the rightful king of France. It was her divine duty to help him take his place on the throne.

The country was in the midst of the Hundred Years' War, waged between the royal houses of England and France—the Battle of Agincourt in 1415 had seen the English beat the French forces and strengthen their position. By the time Joan met Charles in 1429, Henry VI, while still a child, was king of England and France. She was only a teenager, but she persuaded Charles to let her join the French at the sieged city of Orléans, which she helped to liberate. More victories followed and support for *La Pucelle* (the Maid) grew. In July that year, as Joan had prophesized, Charles VII was crowned king of France in Reims.

Hard-line Heretic

It wasn't long before the tide turned for jubilant Joan, and in 1430, after a few military defeats, she was captured by Frenchmen loyal to the English king and handed over to an ecclesiastical court in Rouen. At first there were seventy charges against her, including sorcery, but Joan refused to confess, and after she appeared in court in 1431 and ably defended herself, most of the charges were dropped. Twelve remained, and they largely related to the fact that she wore men's clothing, which she'd been ordered not to do by royal decree. She also said that God had spoken to her directly, which was considered blasphemous. She was offered life imprisonment in exchange for a signed confession and a promise that she would change her ways, which she signed (possibly without realizing what she was admitting to). But a few days later she was still wearing men's clothes and claiming that God had spoken to her. These were the two reasons she was burned at the stake on May 30, 1431.

Which religious leader was known as the Dancing Goddess?

As the forty-four-year Meji era came to an end in 1912, Japan was a nation transformed. It was a time of industrial expansion, foreign influence, and the formation of a modern state with national institutions. Soon people in post-war Japan began to adopt Western fashions, food, and entertainment. There was also a hunger for a new kind of religion.

Celebrity Gods

Feeling unconnected to the long-established Shintō and Buddhist traditions, some people turned to a wave of new religions. Two of the most notorious were founded by women who were criticized by the government's puppet media as being "celebrity gods." One of these was Jiu, founded by spiritualist group member Nagaoka Ryōko. She changed her name to Jikō Son and called for international renewal under the emperor's leadership. One famous follower was sumo grand champion Futabayama, who defended Jikō Son in a physical altercation with police when the Jiu headquarters were raided in 1947. He later left the faith, taking its credibility with him.

Dancing Religion

But Jiu wasn't the only option for those in need of a charismatic, female-led faith. Tenshō Kōtai Jingū-kyō, meaning Religion of the Shrine of the Heavenly Goddess, was founded by Kitamura Sayo, a farmer's wife from the Yamaguchi prefecture. In 1945 she claimed to have been possessed by a deity similar to the Shintō sun goddess Amaterasu Ōmikami. Kitamura Sayo said the goddess had made her shrine

inside her to help save the world by promoting peace. Kitamura Sayo condemned organized religion and governments as "maggot beggars" and led her followers with rousing sermons, singing, and ecstatic dancing, earning the religion the alternative name Odoru Shūkyō or "Dancing Religion." She traveled widely, winning followers in Europe and the Americas, and claimed that she had healing powers and could perform miracles. She became known as the Dancing Goddess and was venerated as a living god. When she died in 1967, her granddaughter took over as leader of the religion. By the early 2000s, there were nearly 500,000 followers across Japan and around the world.

Starting from Scratch

While women have always played an important part in the world's religions, here are some who took things to the next level and became leaders . . . British-born **ANN LEE** brought the Shaking Quaker movement (or Shakers, as they became known, because of the violent shaking that took place while they worshipped) to the United States. She made the decision to leave England in 1774 after having a grand vision in which she was revealed to be the female successor to Jesus. From then on, she was referred to as Mother Ann.

MARY EDDY BAKER accrued a vast fortune and founded the First Church of Christ, Scientist (Christian Science), which was first incorporated in 1879. The religion was based on the idea that disease was an illusion that could be overcome by the science of Christianity.

The Seventh-day Adventist Church, a Protestant Christian denomination, was in part founded by **ELLEN GOULD WHITE**, who experienced visions in childhood and throughout her life. The denomination was notable for its observation of the Sabbath and strong belief in the imminent second coming of Christ.

What is a "walking marriage"?

On the banks of Lugu Lake, bordering the Chinese provinces of Sichuan and Yunnan, lie the villages of the Mosuo people, an ancient ethnic group said to be the last matrilineal society in China.

Meet the Mosuo

Some 40,000 Mosuo inhabit the region today, living in picturesque villages. Their home is remote—they live 8,860 feet above sea level and the nearest city is six hours' drive away—so until relatively recently their customs and cultural practices remained unchanged for centuries. Now tourists travel to the remote area not only for the stunning scenery but also to observe the matrilineal and semimatriarchal lifestyle of the locals. In Mosuo culture, women are the *dabu*, or head of the household, and family names are passed down through the mother's line, rather than the father's.

Marital Bliss

The Mosuo are famous for the cultural practice of *zouhun*, or "walking marriage." Traditionally, once women come of age, they are free to choose their own partners, having as many or as few as they wish. Male lovers, known as *axia*, visit their partner's home on invitation, and a hat is placed on her door to indicate to other men not to enter. Many of these "marriages" result in typical long-lasting relationships, with the difference being that the couple never live together—men and women live with their own mothers and siblings rather than romantic partners. And any children that result from a relationship, be it a

BUDDHISM AND DOG YEARS

Unlike a lot of neighboring cultures, the Mosuo believe in the idea of a "Mother Goddess" rather than a male warrior god. Their traditional Daba faith is also influenced by Tibetan Buddhism. Dogs are venerated in the community—a popular myth is that dogs once had a long lifespan, while humans only lived for thirteen years. The dogs agreed to trade with the humans as long as the humans promised to respect the dogs in return.

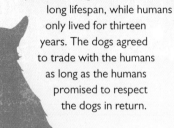

one-night stand or a long partnership, are raised by the mother. Men contribute to the care and financial responsibility of their sisters' children (their nieces and nephews) rather than their own.

Men still have power in Mosuo society, both politically and financially, but it is the women, as the head of the house, who tend to make the decisions about a family's resources. And property and wealth are passed through the mother upon death. This female freedom and autonomy made a lot of sense in the past, when men were frequently absent—traveling long distances in trade caravans to sell produce. And as women are not dependent on their partner for income or social status, when the relationship has run its course, there is no shame in "divorce" and no arguments over money or property. However, with more outside influence, the younger Mosuo are becoming increasingly integrated with the Han Chinese (China's largest ethnic group), with many choosing to forgo the "walking marriage" lifestyle in favor of the cohabiting marriage more common elsewhere in the country.

What's so special about Mother Teresa's habit?

Recognizable in her white habit with three distinctive blue stripes, Mother Teresa dedicated the majority of her life to helping India's poorest people. But the clothes she wore bear an unusual distinction—they've been trademarked in India, the first uniform there to receive intellectual property rights.

• Sister Mary Teresa

Mother Teresa of Calcutta was born Agnes Gonxha Bojaxhiu in 1910. Her family was Albanian and lived in Skopje, now the capital city of Macedonia. Catholicism was a huge part of her early life and she became a nun at the age of sixteen. She left home and joined the Sisters of Loreto in Ireland two years later. That's where she received the name Sister Mary Teresa. The order was known for its missionary work. Shortly after joining, Sister Teresa set off for Calcutta (now Kolkata) for the first time in 1929. There she taught at a school for girls and made her Final Profession of Vows in 1937. She spent twenty years with the order, but became all too aware of the poverty beyondthe gates of the convent. And one day in 1946 she received a "call within a call" to establish her own religious community, the Missionaries of Charity, to minister to the poorest of the poor.

A Sari with a Mission

After two years of preparation, she finally left the Loreto convent to embark on this new journey. Before she did, she removed her religious habit and replaced it with a white cotton veil with a single blue stripe and white tunic. It's believed she chose this simple dress with a touch of blue for its symbolism of purity and the Virgin Mary, but it was also the color of the sari worn by the poorest women who swept the city's streets. Sister Teresa received permission from Rome to wear the garb and would later replace it with a three-striped version, which by then was worn by all the Missionaries of Charity sisters. The religious order was established in 1950 and it was around this time that the other nuns started calling her Mother Teresa.

WEAVING WORKWEAR

For over thirty years, the saris worn by the Missionaries of Charity nuns have been woven by residents at Gandhiji Prem Nivas, a home for leprosy patients on the outskirts of Kolkata. The home was established in 1979 and has grown to become a working welfare home for more than 400 men and women. They produce around 4,000 hand-woven saris every year to clothe more than 5,000 women working as nuns in over 130 countries.

Mother Teresa died in 1997, a Nobel Prize winner and international icon of charitable work and piety. After her death, her religious order continued their good work wearing the same clothes. In 2016 on the same day Mother Teresa was canonized by the Pope, the Indian Trade Marks Registry recognized the blue-bordered sari as intellectual property of the Missionaries of Charity. It was trademarked to prevent "unfair" use by people for commercial purposes.

What did Gracia Mendes Nasi smuggle on her spice ships?

Religious persecution forced her to flee her country of birth, but Gracia Mendes Nasi still risked her life to help others, becoming one of the most successful businesswomen and influential Sephardic Jewish figures of the sixteenth century.

Secret Faith

Little is known of Gracia Mendes Nasi's early life. She was born in Portugal in 1510 and her parents were *conversos*—Jews expelled from Spain in 1492 and then forced to convert to Catholicism. As an adult, Nasi married Francisco Mendes Benveniste, a wealthy spice trader. They had a public Catholic wedding but a private Jewish ceremony with the rituals of their true faith. Unfortunately, her husband died shortly after, leaving her half of his business empire, which she helped to run successfully with her brother-in-law and then on her own after his death.

Underground and Across the Sea

In 1536, the family was forced to flee again as the Pope ordered that a Portuguese Inquisition be established to root out "New Christians" who were still practicing Judaism in secret. They moved initially to the Netherlands, which was more tolerant of *conversos*, and it was here that Nasi set up an underground operation to help others flee persecution. Jews and *conversos* from Portugal and Spain were smuggled in her company's trading ships to Antwerp. She would then give them money and arrange onward travel to the Ottoman Empire, where they could live freely as Jews. Eventually she would make the journey herself after charges were brought against her deceased husband, leaving her and her fortune vulnerable. She made her way to Venice and Ferrara, where, in 1549, she practiced her faith openly for the first time.

Why must some women marry a tree before their wedding?

In Hindu culture, if you are born under the *manglik* star or the mangal dosha, meaning the planet Mars is placed in a certain position on your astrological chart, you are considered to be Mars-cursed.

Written in the Stars

Astrology has an important place in Hindu culture. Some Hindus believe that the heavenly bodies have a significant influence on their lives on earth and that your horoscope or *jyotisha* chart, which is based on the precise time and place of you birth, should be used to help make important decisions, such as who you should marry. Because Mars is an aggressive planet, if you are born under its influence, this could mean you're prone to a combative temperament—not the ideal disposition for a successful marriage. Some even believe that it could lead to divorce or your spouse dying young.

Marrying a Pot

However, the ancient priests came up with a solution. As the curse was thought only to relate to a first marriage, they advised that *manglik* women marry something else first—such as a tree—so that the marriage to their husband would in fact be their second marriage, free from the curse. Known as *kumbh vivaha* or "pot marriage," this practice sees women being ceremoniously married to a peepal or banana tree (or sometimes a statue of the god Vishnu). While it's been widely condemned as derogatory and against the Indian constitution, the practice persists. In 2007 the Indian film star and former Miss World Aishwarya Rai was taken to court by human rights groups for endorsing the practice after it was reported she had undergone the ritual in the lead up to her marriage to Bollywood actor Abhishek Bachchan.

Who is the only Australian to be recognized as a saint by the Catholic church?

In 2010, at Saint Peter's Basilica in Rome, Pope Benedict XVI held a canonization mass that was live-streamed around the world. Around 8,000 Australians had traveled to the Vatican City for the momentous event, because Mary MacKillop was the first person from their home country to be recognized as a saint by the Catholic Church.

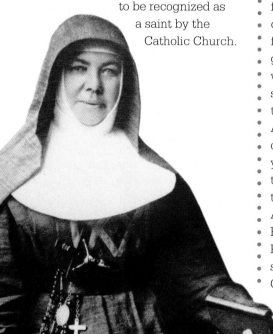

Following in her Father's Footsteps

Born in 1842 in Melbourne, MacKillop was the first of eight children. As a young man, her Scottish father had studied to become a priest, but had opted not to pursue the profession, choosing a life in Australia and fatherhood instead. MacKillop's childhood wasn't always easy—her father struggled to support his growing brood, and as a result they were often on the move or forced to stay with relatives. It was rare for all the siblings to be under the same roof. As Mary grew older, she took on a lot of responsibilities, parenting her younger siblings and earning a living to support them—first as a clerk and then, in 1860, as a governess in South Australia. It was there that she met Father Julian Woods, who ran the Penola Mission. He had decided to set up a religious order to provide Catholic schooling to the local children, many of whom were poor Aborigines with little formal education.

Education for All

In 1866, MacKillop, now in her mid-twenties, took charge of the school and became the first Sister of St. Joseph (Australia's first Catholic order). They were known as the Josephites. The schools were distinctive for their openness—any child was welcome, even those who couldn't afford to attend, and all children were treated equally. They also opened orphanages, homeless shelters, and women's refuges. The Josephites were different from other nuns. They came from less educated, poorer backgrounds and were happy to live as those they helped, often in the outback, relying on others for charity. Some members of the church, unused to their more community-spirited approach, eyed them suspiciously and wanted the rules they lived by to be changed.

Facing Excommunication

The Josephites' biggest test came in 1870 when the nuns reported accusations of child sexual abuse committed by a priest. The offending priest was sent back to Ireland, but one of his friends, another priest, was incensed and convinced the bishop to make the nuns change their constitution (the rules they lived by). When MacKillop refused to accept the changes in 1871, the bishop excommunicated her and the sisters were evicted from their Adelaide convent. For a time she lived in hiding, forbidden to have contact with the church she loved. The following year, however, on his death bed, the bishop arranged for the excommunication to be lifted and the Sisters of St Joseph resumed their social and educational work under her leadership. MacKillop took an active role, eventually being elected Superior General of the congregation and visiting nearly all of the order's convents across Australia and New Zealand before a stroke left her wheelchair-bound. When she died in 1909, there were more than 600 Josephite sisters working across twelve charitable institutions and 117 schools.

How could Victorian women communicate with a flick of the wrist?

The simple fan originally developed as a cooling and insect-repelling device, but by the nineteenth-century it was a fashion must-have most wealthy women wouldn't leave home without. What your fan said about you was one thing, but what you could use your fan to say to somebody else was a different issue entirely.

Function and Fashion

Pictorial records reveal that fans have been around since 3000 BC—they were popular with the Ancient Greeks, Romans, Egyptians, and in China and India, used for ceremonial purposes as well as keeping cool. Handheld fans started to appear in Europe in 1600; they were status symbols for royalty, made from the finest materials. The leaves were decorated by esteemed craftsmen and highly ornamented with lace, mother-of-pearl, and gold leaf. They featured elaborate designs commemorating important historic events and depicting popular myths. And ladies were expected to know how to handle their fan in a manner becoming their social station, so as not to appear coquettish or to attract unwanted attention. And the type of fan mattered, too. By the end of the seventeenth century, most well-to-do women would carry folding fans, whereas less well-off women made do with cheaper fixed feather fans.

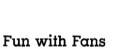

Fun with Fans

Clever fan makers devised ways to make their owners more appealing. In the late 1790s, Charles Francis Badini and Robert Rowe both developed communication fans to allow women to converse across a ballroom, for example. Badini's fan required the user to hold it in one of five positions to indicate specific letters of the alphabet, while Rowe's had each letter printed on a different fold of the fan and the user could point to each letter to spell out a word. Other fans were used for fortune-telling, quizzes, or drinking games, with instructions or questions printed onto the fan itself.

Fanning the Flames

There is a popular myth that by the Victorian age women had developed a complex "secret" fan language as a way to communicate with potential suitors. Although this would have been useful at a time when overt affection or rejection was deemed socially unacceptable, it relied on the men they encountered knowing the secret language, too. The myth's origin was somewhat of a marketing exercise. In 1827, fans were out of fashion and Parisian fan maker Jean-Pierre Duvelleroy was determined to bring them back. He published a leaflet that explained the secret language, which he'd translated from a Spanish text by a man named Fenella, and it was a great success. A ball thrown by the Duchesse de Berry, complete with Duvelleroy fans, saw his business surge, and soon he was supplying Queen Victoria and a whole host of other royals. Duvelleroy's list of gestures included drawing the fan across the cheek for "I love you" and twirling in the right hand for "I love another." While these signals were probably used more in a tongue-in-cheek sense, versions of this fan language were reprinted in contemporary books and popular magazines across Europe.

What was Jarena Lee called to do?

Jarena Lee's 1836 book, *The Life and Religious Experience of Jarena Lee*, was the first published autobiography by an African-American woman. Her religious experience led her to the African Methodist Episcopal Church, where she became the faith's first officially recognized female preacher.

Finding her Faith

Lee was born in Cape May, New Jersey, on February 11, 1783, to free black parents. They may have been free, but they were poor, and at the age of seven, Lee was sent to work as a domestic servant for a white family sixty miles

from the home she knew. While she received no formal education, she taught herself to read and write. Her first experiences with Christianity were within the white community she worked in and largely negative— segregated churches were the norm and she felt like she didn't belong, despite her growing spirituality. As an adult she moved to Philadelphia and found the African Methodist Episcopal Church, being baptized there aged twenty-four. Around 1811 she felt called by God to preach, but the minister told her women weren't allowed.

Called by God Again

She might never have taken up the pulpit. Eight years passed, and in that time Lee had married a preacher and become a mother. But by 1818 her husband had died, and it was shortly after that she felt called by God again. Bishop Richard Allen gave her permission to hold prayer meetings and she became an exhorter (a member of the congregation who shares their personal conversion story). Then one day she was attending a service at Mother Bethel Church in Philadelphia when part-way through his sermon the visiting preacher was unable to

continue. It was Lee who stood up and finished it for him, moving the congregation with her passion. Bishop Allen was also present, and in her autobiography Lee described how he rose up after her sermon and said, "He now as much believed that I was called to that work, as any of the preachers present." This was the permission Lee so desperately wanted, and she embarked on a career as a traveling minister, preaching across the country's northeast.

The Second Great Awakening

Lee's awakening coincided with what later became known as the "Second Great Awakening," a period of intense Protestant fervor between 1790 and 1840, when churches held revival meetings and converted thousands of people. Many of these converts were women who were most heavily impacted by the social and economic changes facing the country—the new sects encouraged spiritual enlightenment, no matter one's gender, race, or social status. Even so, Lee faced opposition and discrimination as a black woman preacher. Many still felt that women shouldn't be allowed to preach. She would arrive in towns where the church doors would be locked so she couldn't enter. Often, she would find a nearby hall and carry out her ministry, only to win the locals round. Later she traveled further afield to places where slavery was still legal and used theology to argue against the abomination.

How many hymns did Fanny Crosby write?

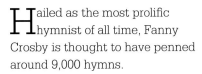

Hailed as the most prolific hymnist of all time, Fanny Crosby is thought to have penned around 9,000 hymns.

Young Poet

Born in New York in 1820, Crosby had a more difficult start than most. When she was just six weeks old, an unqualified doctor applied mustard paste to her eyes in an attempt to cure a cold. The cold cleared up, but she was left blinded. Shortly after that her father died and her mother had to fend for them both. Fanny started writing poetry when she was just eight years old and learned huge passages of the Bible by heart. Later, her luck changed with the opening of the newly founded New York Institute for the Blind, which she attended for twelve years; she went on to become a teacher there.

Praise the Lord

Her talent for poetry was obvious, and when she was twenty-three she recited her work at the U.S. Senate (where she also urged politicians to support education for the blind). In the late 1850s, after resigning from teaching and marrying a talented organist, Crosby started to write hymn lyrics instead. She had a deal with a publisher to submit three hymns a week but often sent in six or seven. Among her most popular hymns are "Safe in the Arms of Jesus," "Blessed Assurance," and "To God Be the Glory." The precise number of Crosby hymns is unknown as many were published under pseudonyms. In 1905, ten years before her death, the Methodist Church started recognizing March 26 as Fanny Crosby Day.

RELIGION AND CULTURE

Keep the faith and trust your instincts—here are some quick teasers to test you and your knowledge of these cultural quirks and religious tales.

Questions

1. What was the name of the Irish order that Mother Teresa joined?

2. Why was Indian film star and former Miss World Aishwarya Rai taken to court by human rights groups in 2007?

3. How many of the original seventy charges leveled at Joan of Arc was she actually found guilty of?

4. What religion was Gracia Mendes Nasi's family forced to convert to?

5. Why was nun Mary MacKillop inspired by her father?

6. In the Mosuo culture, what are *axia*?

7. What is thought to have caused Fanny Crosby's blindness?

8. Which religious leader traveled to America in 1774 after having a vision that she was Jesus's successor?

9. What is the period of intense Protestant fervor in North America between 1790 and 1840 known as?

10. According to Jean-Pierre Duvelleroy's fan language, what would it mean if someone drew their fan across their cheek?

Turn to page 215 for the answers.

WHO WAS JAPAN'S FIRST TRUE GENERAL?

WHICH PRINCESS OWNED 10,000 HORSES?

WHY DID BOUDICCA LEAD A REBEL FORCE AGAINST THE ROMANS?

WHO WAS SADIE THE GOAT, AND WHAT HAPPENED TO HER EAR?

WARRIORS AND SUPERWOMEN

WHICH WOMAN STRUCK OUT TWO OF HISTORY'S GREATEST BASEBALL PLAYERS?

Who was Japan's first true general?

When we imagine Japanese warriors, we picture male samurai dressed in ornate armor wielding long swords against their enemies. But even as far back as AD 200 there were women, the *onna-bugeisha*, who fought alongside the men, leading armies and protecting their communities.

Smarts and Sword Skills

The *onna-bugeisha* can be traced back to Empress Jingū—a skilled fighter who orchestrated and led a conquest to Korea in the third century AD. At a time when cultural norms saw women as second to men, with most carrying out housework and motherhood duties, the *onna-bugeisha* were part of the samurai, a noble military class in feudal Japan. Revered as powerful and highly educated women, they were warriors in their own right. As well as studying science and literature, they learned a traditional martial art called *tantōjutsu*, still practiced today, and how to wield a *ko-naginata*. This long pole-like weapon featured a deadly blade at one end. It was smaller than the similar *ō-naginata* favored by male warriors, to allow for a female fighter's stature and strength. *Onna-bugeisha* would also carry a double-edged *kaiken* dagger at all times, even if they married and moved in with a husband. The ten-inch blade could be used for self-defense in tight spaces. It also had ceremonial uses, such as ritual suicide.

Generally Speaking . . .

Many *onna-bugeisha* were the protectors of their local villages, especially in communities where men were scarce. And when wars occurred between rival clans, they fought alongside male warriors

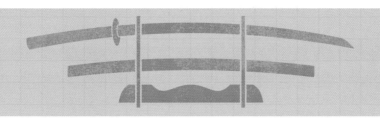

or in their own distinct army. In 1180, such a war broke out between the Minamoto and the Taira clans. Fighting for the Minamoto throughout the five-year Genpei War, was General Tomoe Gozen, an *onna-bugeisha* of exceptional talent. A skilled archer and rider, she had mastered the *katana* sword, the iconic weapon favored by the samurai. Her troops were loyal and trusted her command. Toward the end of the war, in 1184, she led 300 warriors into battle against a 2,000-strong Tiara force. Only five Minamoto fighters survived, including Tomoe Gozen. Her notoriety and success on the battlefield led the Minamoto master to declare her Japan's first true general. The *onna-bugeisha* thrived for centuries after, with more and more women taking up arms to protect their clans from invasion.

The Last *Onna-bugeisha*

In 1868, the Boshin War saw the Imperial Court facing off against the Tokugawa shogunate. There was unrest among the people, some of whom were dissatisfied with the economic downturn under the shogunate's rule and wanted power to be restored to the Imperial Court. On the shogunate side a special army, made up of *onna-bugeisha*, and later named the *Joshitai*, was led by Nakano Takeko. At the Battle of Aizu, the *onna-bugeishas'* last stand, she fought bravely but was shot during the battle. With her last breath she asked her sister to cut off her head so the enemy couldn't take her body as a trophy. Her sister complied and buried Nakano Takeko's head under a pine tree at a nearby temple. Nakano Takeko is said to have been Japan's last great female warrior.

Why did Boudicca lead a rebel force against the Romans?

The Iceni tribe, led by King Prasutagus, controlled the east of England in modern-day Norfolk. When the Romans invaded England in AD 43, they left the Iceni alone, but a few years later when the king died, the Romans saw their chance to take over.

A Woman Scorned

Boudicca was Prasutagus's wife, and the mother of their two daughters. Little is known about her, and the earliest written evidence of her existence comes from a Roman historian writing fifty years after her death. Her name comes from the Celtic word "*bouda*," meaning victory, and is also spelled Boadicea. But it is known that she was a Celt, and in Celtic society women could rule as queens and own property independently of their husbands. Under Roman law, however, women had few rights, especially over their husband's property. When Prasutagus died in AD 60, he had tried to protect his family's future by leaving half of his wealth to the Roman Emperor Nero. He hoped this voluntary gesture would appease the Romans and safeguard Boudicca's position as Queen of the Iceni.

In reality, Prasutagus's wishes were ignored. The Romans annexed the Iceni kingdom and confiscated the property of the tribe's chiefs. For Boudicca a worse fate awaited: She was stripped and flogged, and her two daughters were raped and beaten by Roman soldiers. The humiliation of their queen caused widespread anger and resentment among the Iceni toward the Romans. Hurt, humiliated, but not willing to give in, Boudicca formed an alliance with the Trinovantes, a neighboring tribe, and prepared for battle.

Boudicca in Battle

While the Roman provincial governor, Gaius Suetonius Paullinus, was away in the west, leading a military campaign in North Wales, Boudicca saw her chance. Her amassed army of rebels attacked the British Roman capital, Camulodunum (now Colchester), and defeated the Roman Ninth Legion, destroying the city. They marched onward to Londinium and Verulamium (London and St. Albans), burning military outposts as they went and slaughtering 70,000 Roman soldiers and supporters.

Crushing the Rebellion

The Celts were a terrifying force, but they'd had the element of surprise. But when Paullinus returned, they faced the full force of the Roman army. Unlike the Roman soldiers with their body armor, javelins, and short swords, which were ideal for close-combat, the Celts wore no armor and wielded long swords that needed space to inflict real damage. The last stand is believed to have taken place near what is now Milton Keynes on Watling Street, an important Roman road. The Celts were overconfident, and many people had traveled to watch the battle, their wagons blocking the Celts' retreat route. As the Roman machine began to overpower them, the Celts had nowhere to run and in the confined space of battle were quickly finished off.

Boudicca must have known her fate was sealed—she had defied the Romans and led a rebellion. If she didn't die on the battlefield, then to avoid capture and torture, she most likely poisoned herself shortly after the Celts' defeat. Her final resting place is still unknown.

Who was Sadie the Goat, and what happened to her ear?

Gang leader Sadie Farrell lived in late nineteenth-century New York City's notorious Fourth Ward neighborhood. She got her unusual nickname because of her signature move—choosing to head-butt people when she mugged them. But her bad behavior caught up with her when fellow female gangster Gallus Mag, a six-foot-tall bouncer, bit off her ear in a vicious fight. That's when Sadie the Goat turned to piracy.

Sailing Sadie

Farrell needed to lay low and steer clear of Mag, so she gathered a group of bandits, some of whom were members of the infamous Charlton Street Gang, and stole a ship. They flew a Jolly Roger, the iconic pirate flag, and took to the waters of the Hudson and Harlem rivers. They sailed up and down, causing trouble and raiding the riverfront farm houses and mansions. Sometimes they even took people aboard and held them hostage for ransom money. But after a while, their escapades proved less profitable and far more risky when the farmers got tired of their antics and started shooting at them from the riverbank. Now known as Queen of the Waterfront, Farrell returned to her Fourth Ward roost and went back to her old ways. At some point she made peace with Mag, who handed her back her ear (she'd pickled it as a souvenir). Farrell is believed to have worn it in a locket around her neck for the rest of her life.

Warrior Women of the High Seas

Real-life buccaneers like Blackbeard and the Barbarossa brothers may have come to epitomize the idea of the gold-smuggling, port-plundering pirate, but there were a number of women from history who would have proudly proclaimed "A pirate's life for me!" Here are just a few . . .

ANNE BONNY was a red-haired Irishwoman who thrived during the golden age of piracy in the Caribbean, which lasted from the 1650s to the 1730s. She came from a respectable family, but her father disowned her when she married a pirate. He would've been shocked to learn she left her husband for an even more notorious swashbuckler: John "Calico Jack" Rackham. Her best friend was **MARY READ**, who had dressed as a man to join the British military and was forced into piracy when her ship was attacked en route to the West Indies. Both women were captured for their exploits in 1720, but while Bonny was spared the hangman's noose because she was pregnant, Read died from fever in her prison cell.

In 1801, after Bonny and Read's heyday, a Chinese prostitute called Shi Xiang Gu was captured by pirates and ended up marrying the Red Flag Fleet's fearsome leader Zheng Yi. When he died six years later, she moved to take over the fleet of 300 ships and up to 40,000 men. Then known as Ching Shih, she helped to grow the fleet to six times its size, ruling over her vast floating domain and army with her own rules and tax laws. She retired in 1810, this time marrying her first mate and settling down on dry land to enjoy her wealth.

What was Annie Edson Taylor's wooden barrel used for?

Annie Edson Taylor had led a pretty conventional life until she was widowed in 1863 by the American Civil War. She moved all over the United States doing odd jobs before settling in Michigan, where she opened a finishing school. But when she read that the Pan-American Exposition was happening in nearby Buffalo, New York, she had an idea to earn a few bucks.

Barrel of Courage

The expo would provide a large audience for what she was planning—going over Niagara Falls in a wooden barrel. She was sixty-three years old, and understandably people were concerned she might injure herself or even die, so a cat was sent down in a barrel first to see how it fared. After the successful feline trial on October 24 (which happened to be her birthday) in 1901, Taylor was strapped into a five-foot-high barrel lined with cushions. The barrel was sealed and filled with air using a bike pump. The crowds watched as she was towed out into the river and cut loose. There was no going back.

The barrel soon plummeted over the edge of Horseshoe Falls (the largest of the Niagara Falls), appearing about twenty minutes later downstream. People watched in amazement as Taylor emerged from the barrel, a little bruised and concussed, but very much alive. Unfortunately, the fame and fortune she hoped for were not forthcoming. But her bravery did inspire others to take the plunge. Under the Niagara Parks Act, it is illegal to perform a stunt or feat with the park without written permission from the Parks Commission. In the years since Taylor's leap of faith, an estimated 15 people have attempted similar stunts, with only 10 surviving.

Why were the Nazis terrified of Lyudmila Pavlichenko?

As one of the Red Army's deadliest snipers, Lyudmila Pavlichenko racked up 309 official kills during World War II, including one hundred German officers. She was so effective, the Soviets sent her to America to drum up support for the war.

Shoot to Kill

Born in 1916 in Ukraine, Pavlichenko was an unruly tomboy who hated to be beaten. She learned to shoot from a young age, so when Germany invaded the Soviet Union in 1941, she put herself forward to join the army. Women weren't allowed in, but she managed to get an "audition" of sorts where she proved her marksmanship skills. She joined the Red Army's 25th Rifle Division and served in Odessa, Moldavia, Sevastopol, and the Crimean Peninsula. Her assignments included counter-sniping, where she engaged in drawn-out duels with enemy snipers, including one that lasted for three days. She was shot four times but was only pulled from active duty after taking shrapnel to the face. She then took on the role of training other snipers.

Touring with the First Lady

In 1942, aged twenty-five, Pavlichenko was sent to the United States to rally support for a "second front" in Europe to take the pressure off the Soviets. She was the first Soviet citizen to be welcomed to the White House, where she met President Franklin Roosevelt and First Lady Eleanor Roosevelt. The latter invited Pavlichenko to join her on a speaking tour of the country to tell Americans about her time in combat. The two reportedly became good friends, with Roosevelt visiting Pavlichenko fifteen years later when she toured Moscow.

Which woman struck out two of history's greatest baseball players?

On April 2, 1931, New York Yankees legend Babe Ruth stepped up to the plate in front of a 4,000-strong crowd in Chattanooga, Tennessee. The Yankees were playing an exhibition game against the city's Class AA minor-league team, the Lookouts. So far, so good. But facing Ruth to pitch on the mound was the Lookouts' latest signing, a seventeen-year-old girl by the name of Jackie Mitchell.

Let's Play Ball!

Mitchell had grown up in Memphis with Baseball Hall of Fame's Dazzy Vance as her neighbor. He'd shown her the ropes, teaching her how to pitch, and she was hooked. When her family moved to Chattanooga, she joined a baseball school, where she was renowned for her sinking curveball. Then she attracted the attention of Lookouts' president Joe Engel, who signed her to the team. She is believed to be the first woman to receive a professional baseball contract.

Legendary Lookout

The Yankees' batting line-up at the time of the exhibition game was known as "Murderer's Row" and is widely considered one of the best in baseball history. Swapped in as a relief pitcher, Mitchell faced off against Ruth. He let the first pitch pass for a ball, then proceeded to swing and miss three times for a strikeout, throwing down his bat in disgust. Lou Gehrig was up next, and Mitchell's three pitches resulted in another three swings and misses. The local crowd went wild, although the Yankees did go on to win the game 14–4. Mitchell's Lookouts contract was terminated shortly after the game, adding to the speculation that her hiring

A LEAGUE OF THEIR OWN

While women had been playing baseball, particularly in traveling squads known as barnstormers, since the later nineteenth century, it wasn't until 1943 that they finally got their own league. With so many men leaving the ball park for the battlefield in World War II, baseball business was at risk. So for twelve seasons, more than 600 female players of the All-American Girls Professional Baseball League (AAGPBL) filled stadiums across the United States, keeping fans of the game entertained until 1954, when it was disbanded.

a noted showman, willing to stop at nothing for a bit of publicity—he once traded his shortstop for a turkey, which he then had killed, cooked, and served up to sportswriters. Mitchell's debut for the club certainly pulled in the punters and attracted national attention for the team. But if it was a set-up, Ruth and Gehrig never said so, and Mitchell always maintained that she had defeated the players fair and square.

was just for the publicity, although she did continue to play baseball until 1937 with various amateur and touring teams. The Yankees would go on to win the 1932 World Series and continue to dominate baseball for the next four decades.

Pitching for Publicity?

The game was originally set for April 1, and some suspect that signing Mitchell (a week before the game) and putting her on the mound was Engel's idea of an April Fool's Day prank to send ticket sales soaring. Others speculated that the Yankees were in on the joke, deliberately striking out. Engel was

Which princess owned 10,000 horses?

She was a princess and the great-great-granddaughter of the mighty conqueror Genghis Khan—an attractive prospect for any thirteenth-century Mongolian man. But Khutulun wasn't interested in a husband, unless he could beat her in a contest befitting a true warrior.

From Fighting Stock

Born in 1260, Khutulun was a trained fighter and accompanied her father Khaidu Khan, a descendent of the royal family, on the battlefield. Like many Mongolian women at the time, she learned how to shoot a bow and arrow, ride horses, and wrestle alongside her fourteen brothers. Italian explorer and writer Marco Polo described her as "so strong and brave that in all her father's realm there was no man who could outdo her in feats of strength." Her parents wanted her to marry, but she wouldn't settle for anyone inferior to her. So she proposed an idea: If a suitor could beat her in a challenge of endurance, physical strength, or military skill, she would marry him. But if he lost, he had to gift her one hundred horses. Despite the risk involved, there was no shortage of men willing to put their finest steeds on the line in pursuit of the princess's hand. But none were able to beat her. She is said to have accumulated 10,000 horses through these various marriage contests.

have lost so much, the prince took off, leaving his horses behind. It's thought she eventually did get married to a man of her choosing, although sources disagree on this. But unlike other women of the period, she is known more for her skills in combat and archery than for the deeds of her husband or sons.

Family Feud

In its heyday, the Mongolian Empire was vast, covering huge swathes of China, Europe, and the Middle East. But by the time Khutulun was born, there were divisions among Genghis Khan's descendants. Khutulun's father, Khaidu, controlled large parts of Central Asia, while his cousin Khubilai Khan was the fifth *khagan* or ruler of the Mongol Empire. Khaidu wanted to preserve his nomadic lifestyle, while Khubilai was trying to keep control of the empire and develop long-distance trade routes through Central Asia. Over a thirty-year territorial war, Khutulun went on a number of military expeditions with her father, impressing him with her bravery, pride, physical strength, and endurance.

Betting Big

One story goes that in 1260, a rich, handsome, and skillful prince arrived to try and win Khutulun's hand. He was confident, too, betting 1,000 horses instead of the requisite one hundred, to best her in a wrestling match. Her parents took her to the side and tried to convince her to throw the fight—they felt the prince was a worthy husband and she should let him win. But Khutulun refused to succumb to her parents' wishes and readily accepted the prince's challenge. When the time came to wrestle, they were equally skilled and it was probably a close call, but Khutulun soon overcame the suitor and won the match. Embarrassed to have been beaten by a woman and to

What did the "White Mouse," "Lise," and the "Limping Lady" have in common?

While it was rare to see women on the frontlines of World War II, many played a vital role as undercover operatives, particularly in the final years of the conflict as the Allied forces prepared for D-Day. Nancy Wake, Odette Sansom, and Virginia Hall were three such remarkable women, although they were known by other names.

Quiet As a Mouse

As a twenty-year-old Australian nurse Nancy Wake traveled from her home in Australia to New York, London, and Paris, where she eventually settled and worked as a journalist. She even interviewed Adolf Hitler in 1933. A couple of months after the Allies declared war on Germany, she married a wealthy French industrialist and together they joined the French resistance, helping to smuggle Jews and Allied pilots out of the country. In 1943 she trained with the French section of the British Special Operations Executive (SOE) in England. One of just thirty-nine women and 430 men, she was parachuted back into France in 1944 and organized

drops of weapons and equipment in preparation for D-Day. Then she led an army of 7,000 guerrilla fighters against Nazi troops in northern Auvergne. She was on the Gestapo's wanted list and they called her the "White Mouse" for her elusive tactics. The world called her a hero and she became the most decorated woman of World War II, receiving Britain's George Medal, America's Medal of Freedom, and France's Legion of Honor, among other awards.

Agent S.23

Odette Sansom, a Frenchwoman and mother living in England, joined the SOE in 1942 after hearing about her family suffering in German-occupied France. She joined the branch's "F section" and became Agent S.23; her codename was Lise. After arriving in

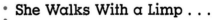

She Walks With a Limp . . .

The first female SOE operative sent to France was American radio operator Virginia Hall. She posed as a *New York Post* reporter and lived in Lyon as a spy for two years. Similarly to Wake, she established resistance networks, helped downed airmen, and located drop zones for weapons and money from the British. She was considered "the most dangerous of all Allied spies" by the Gestapo, who didn't know her identity but referred to her as the "Limping Lady" because of her walk. Hall had an artificial left leg (she'd lost it in a hunting accident years before the war). Later, she joined the U.S. Office of Strategic Services and went back to France as a radio operator, disguising herself as an elderly milkmaid to avoid detection. She carried her radio in a suitcase and sent messages in Morse code to London.

Cannes she joined a resistance group, but her identity was betrayed and she was arrested by the Gestapo. The Nazi's police force used brutal torture techniques—all her toenails were pulled out and they burned her back with a hot poker—but she never revealed her fellow agents' identities. She also spent nearly a year in Ravensbrück concentration camp before the war came to an end. Sansom was the first woman to receive both the George Cross and the Legion of Honor.

Who was the last true Beloved Woman of the Cherokees?

Nanyehi Ward was born around 1738 and lived in Chota, a sacred region of the Cherokee Nation in modern-day eastern Tennessee. A member of the prestigious Wolf Clan—her great-grandfather was Supreme Chief Moytoy of Tellico, a prominent leader—her name would also go on to hold great significance for the Cherokee.

A Devastating Loss

Ward came into the world at a difficult time for her people. English missionaries were trying to live among the Cherokee to convert them to Christianity, meaning their traditional faith and customs were under threat. At the same time, the Cherokee faced hostility from the Muscogee Creeks over territory. When she was a teenager Ward married a mighty warrior, Kingfisher from the Deer Clan. They had two children together, but he wouldn't live to see them grow up. In 1755, the couple rode together in the Battle of Taliwa against the Creeks—it was the war's most deadly battle, and although the Cherokee came out on top, Kingfisher was killed in the fighting. Ward would have been around eighteen years old, but she was as fierce as her husband. She took up his gun and with a rousing war song led her people to victory.

Becoming *Ghigau*

It was after this that her people gave her the title *Ghigau*, or Beloved Woman. The Cherokees believed that supreme beings spoke to the people through the *Ghigau*. This hugely influential position gave Ward a seat on the Council of Chiefs, leadership of the Women's Council, and other important responsibilities. She had to prepare a ceremonial tea given to warriors before battle, and she had the right to decide what happened to prisoners of war. It was rare for such a young woman to be bestowed with the role, but the people felt she had earned it for the bravery and leadership she had shown on the battlefield.

Making Peace and Butter

As more and more white colonists settled on Cherokee land, violating the 1763 Royal Proclamation, which governed the settlement of Americans on Native land, she also took on the duties of peace negotiator. Around 1759 she remarried, this time to Bryant Ward, a white trader, changing her name to Nancy. In June 1776 she heard that three Cherokee war chiefs were planning to attack the illegal white settlements on the Watauga River. She warned the settlers, to try and avoid unnecessary bloodshed, but in July another attack saw a white woman, Lydia Bean, taken prisoner.

She was condemned to burn to death and was tied to a stake on a mound in a Cherokee town. She was condemned to burn to death and was tied to a stake in the center of Tuskegee. But Ward's power as *Ghighua* meant she could grant Bean clemency, and she cut her down and took her into her own home, eventually returning the prisoner to her husband. While recuperating, Bean taught Ward how to churn butter and weave cloth, and introduced her to the idea of farming cattle. She is believed to be one of the first Cherokee to raise a dairy herd.

What has Peggy Whitson done more than any other American?

Raised on a farm in rural Iowa, it was Peggy Whitson's dream to become a NASA astronaut. Little did she know that dream would become a reality in a record-breaking way.

If At First You Don't Succeed

It was 1978 when Whitson was at high school that she learned that NASA had recruited its first female astronauts. (NASA first sent a woman to space in 1983, when Sally Ride was part of the crew for the seventh space shuttle mission.) Whitson eventually joined

NASA as a biochemist, working as a project scientist for the Shuttle-Mir Program, but she had to apply ten times for astronaut training before finally being accepted in 1996.

Breaking Records in Space

In 2002, Whitson, after years of training, went to space for the first time on a six-month expedition to the International Space Station (ISS). While there she became the first NASA Science Officer and carried out twenty-one scientific investigations into human life sciences and microgravity. She would go on to spend two more extended stays on the ISS: one in 2007–08, where she became the station's first female commander, and another in 2016–17, making her the first woman to command the station twice. In between off-earth trips, she served as the organization's first female chief astronaut—the corps' most senior position. And her impressive stats don't stop there. She currently holds the title for the most spacewalks carried out by a woman and has spent more time in space than any other U.S. astronaut—an impressive 665 days (nearly two years of her life!). She retired from NASA in 2018.

WARRIORS AND SUPERWOMEN

They've been launched into space, led their people into battle, faced down Nazi snipers, and traveled by barrel over Niagara Falls. Now all you have to do is answer the questions in this quiz. Easy.

Questions

1. What was the nickname for the Yankees batting line-up that included Babe Ruth and Lou Gehrig?
2. Which city did Boudicca and her rebel army destroy first on their campaign against the Romans?
3. What was the name of the British intelligence branch that Nancy Wake, Odette Sansom, and Virginia Hall were part of?
4. What was notable about Lyudmila Pavlichenko's 1942 visit to the White House?
5. Who was the first female NASA astronaut to go to space?
6. What was sent down Niagara Falls in a barrel before Annie Edison Taylor took the trip herself?
7. How many horses did a suitor need to bet to compete for Khutulun's hand in marriage?
8. Which rivers did Sadie the Goat sail on?
9. Who did the Cherokee face in the Battle of Taliwa?
10. What was the name of the double-edged dagger wielded by *onna-bugeisha*?

Turn to page 215 for the answers.

HOW DID AMERICA'S FIRST FEMALE DETECTIVE HELP FOIL A PRESIDENTIAL ASSASSINATION ATTEMPT?

WHICH RUSSIAN NOBLEWOMAN WAS IMPRISONED FOR KILLING 38 PEOPLE?

DID LIZZIE BORDEN MURDER HER PARENTS?

WHY WAS MIYUKI ISHIKAWA A MURDEROUS MIDWIFE?

WHO WERE THE WILD WOMEN OF THE WILD WEST?

CRIME AND PUNISHMENT

HOW MANY "WITCHES" WERE BURNED AT THE STAKE IN SALEM?

How did America's first female detective help foil a presidential assassination attempt?

The moment when Confederate sympathizer John Wilkes Booth shot Abraham Lincoln at the Ford Theater, Washington, DC, in 1865 is one of the most famous assassinations in American history. But what is less well known is that there was a foiled attempt to kill the president four years prior, and that a woman helped to prevent it.

The Art of Detection

In August 1856, Kate Warne, a young widow, entered the offices of the Pinkerton National Detective Agency in Chicago and asked for a job. She didn't want to be a secretary but a sleuth of the first order. She convinced Allan Pinkerton of her usefulness as a woman, especially for undercover work, and he acquiesced, writing in 1874, "True, it was the first experiment of the sort that had ever been tried; but we live in a progressive age, and in a progressive country." Over her time with the agency she proved her worth, posing as various characters to gather evidence and chase leads. Notably, in 1859, she became Madame Imbert, befriending Belle Maroney, the wife of an Adams Express Company messenger who stole $50,000 from the business. Warne's months-long undercover stint helped to secure much-needed evidence of Nathan Maroney's guilt. She also posed as a fortune-teller, unveiling a murderous poison plot, and even as Pinkerton's own wife to collect military intelligence during the Civil War. But undoubtedly, her most vital role came in 1861 when the agency was hired to protect President-elect Abraham Lincoln.

On the Rails

Initially, the head of the Philadelphia, Wilmington, and Baltimore Railroad contacted Pinkerton believing Washington, DC, might be under attack by secessionists. He'd heard rumors that they planned to prevent the inauguration and use the rail network to thwart Lincoln's travel plans and control all routes in and out of the capital. With the inauguration just six weeks away, Pinkerton's agents, including Warne, infiltrated parties and visited saloons across Baltimore to sniff out the details. Baltimore was where Lincoln would have to change stations, walking a little over a mile before boarding another train for his onward journey. And their assumptions proved correct. Warne, posing as a rich Southern socialist, discovered that the plan was to distract security at Baltimore's Calvert Street Station by breaking into a fight and then surrounding Lincoln in a murderous mob. The detectives had been called in to protect the railroad, but it was the president-elect who needed their help.

Protecting the President

They switched up Lincoln's schedule so he'd arrive into Baltimore in the dead of night, earlier than planned and without his usual entourage. So that he wasn't spotted on the train, Warne helped secure four double berths in the rear sleeper car. She posed as Lincoln's sister and implored the conductor for privacy for her invalid brother. They dressed Lincoln in a shawl with a cane and hat to disguise his distinguishable frame and features. And the plan worked—Lincoln made it to Washington unharmed for his inauguration, and Warne got a promotion to Female Superintendent of Detectives.

Which Russian noblewoman was imprisoned for killing 38 people?

Darya Nikolayevna Saltykova was born into a life of privilege in 1730, a time when Russian nobles ruled the roost and could do no wrong. So when she started taking liberties, and lives, the people were powerless to stop her.

Cruel Mistress

Saltykova married well—to Gleb Alexandrovich Saltykov, captain of the Calvary Regiment of the Russian Imperial Guard. They had two lavish homes—a mansion in Moscow and a summer estate in Troitskoye—and mixed with all the finest families. Gleb died in 1756, leaving Saltykova,

a young widow with two sons, in charge of the family's serfs. Serfs were the peasant laborers who worked for the nobles. Technically they weren't slaves because they could work for their freedom, but their quality of life depended largely on the goodwill of their employer.

Saltykova ran a strict and unsympathetic household. Obsessed with cleanliness and order, she would fly off the handle for the smallest infraction, and progressively her punishments got worse. She kept her maids locked in an empty hut for days and beat the young girls until they bled. Then things turned murderous—the first official complaint against her was that she'd beaten a pregnant girl to death. But despite witnesses' testimony, the police were reluctant to bring any charges. What kind of precedent would it set if they started arresting noblewomen?

Serfs Spill the Beans

The atrocities continued: She set a woman's hair on fire and pushed an eleven-year-old girl down a staircase. And then, after she'd killed Yermolai Ilyin's three wives in turn, she finally got her comeuppance. Saltykova had threatened the stableman, but he'd had enough. He went to the police and presented them with a letter claiming Saltykova had killed over one hundred of her servants. The new Empress Catherine the Great (see page 108) was trying to curb the power of the nobility and show the world that Russia was a humane and enlightened country. When she got word of the accusations, she made sure a thorough investigation took place. Soon charges were brought, and Saltykova stood trial and was found guilty of killing thirty-eight people. She refused to confess and, following a public shaming, was imprisoned for the rest of her life—thirty-three years, eleven of which were spent in an underground cell.

HUNGARY FOR BLOOD

According to the Guinness World Records, the most prolific female murderer was Hungarian noblewoman Elizabeth Báthory. More than a century before Saltykova was mercilessly murdering her serfs, Báthory was lauding over Čachtice Castle in the Carpathian Mountains (present-day Slovakia). She was married to Count Nádasdy and, similarly to Saltykova, after he died rumors surfaced that she'd killed local peasant girls. After an investigation in 1609, it transpired she'd been practicing vampirism, killing virgins, and drinking and bathing in their blood to keep herself looking youthful. More than 600 women are thought to have been slain in pursuit of her unusual habits. While servants who helped her were executed for their involvement, Báthory got off lightly, being confined to her castle until her death in 1614.

Who were the wild women of the Wild West?

Crowd-pleasing shows like Buffalo Bill's Wild West toured America and the world in the late 1800s, with parades, reenactments, sideshows, and sharpshooters like Annie Oakley. But a number of women really did find themselves living way out west on the wrong side of the law.

Heartless Hart

Inspired by the touring shows she'd seen, Canadian mother of two Pearl Hart left her kids and native Toronto to seek the excitement and independence of life in the Wild West. But when she moved to Arizona in the fading years of the nineteenth century, she found a fairly civilized and sedate American Frontier. She worked as a cook but struggled financially.

Then she met Joe Boot, a German farmer, and the two set about mining for silver, unsuccessfully, and robbing men of their money. (Hart would seduce the victim and Boot would storm in and pretend to be a cuckolded husband.) Eventually they came up with a plan to get rich quick. They robbed a stagecoach—although Hart made sure to return one dollar to each of their victims—and were caught four days later. Hart received five years in prison, but she became a local celebrity and her presence at the prison proved disruptive, so she only served eighteen months. Little is known of her fate, but one story goes that she ended up in a touring show just like the ones that had inspired her—a real-life Annie Oakley.

Starr of the Show

In 1880 May Shirley (known as Belle) married Sam Starr, a Cherokee Indian with unsavory associates, including notorious outlaws Jesse James and the Younger brothers. Born in 1848, she'd already survived some turbulent years with Missouri menace Jim Reed, who'd been killed in custody after committing the sensational Austin–San Antonio stagecoach robbery. The Starrs had a ranch in present-day Alabama named Younger's Bend. It was a popular spot for outlaws, which no doubt fueled the Starrs' own criminal exploits. They went to prison for horse theft in 1883, and over the next few years they were indicted, although never convicted, on a number of other charges, including post office robbery. Sam was killed in 1887, and two years later Belle was shot in the back. Her murderer was never caught, but given the company she kept, there were plenty of suspects.

Bloody Bender

The Bloody Benders committed up to twenty-one murders in the area now known as Cherryvale, Kansas. The family of four used fake names and enticed travelers to stay at their inn on the Great Osage Trail. Daughter Kate Bender (real name Eliza Griffith) posed as a spiritual medium, attracting customers with her good looks and psychic abilities. During dinner, a family member would attack the victim with a hammer, before slitting his throat in the cellar and stealing his money. After a series of disappearances, the townsfolk decided to search every property in the area. But the Benders fled before they were caught. At their house, locals found a foul-smelling, blood-soaked cellar and a garden littered with grave sites where the family buried their victims.

How did murderess Belle Gunness lure victims right to her door?

In 1908 Belle Gunness's home burned to the ground and the corpses of a headless woman and three children were found in the rubble. But that wasn't what shocked investigators the most.

Matrimonial Murder

Around 20,000 people flocked to what remained of Gunness's farm in La Porte, Indiana, after it was reported the bodies of twelve men, decomposing and dismembered, were found buried on her property. It transpired that the widowed Gunness had posted matrimonial ads in the local Scandinavian paper to lure innocent bachelors to her farm. There were many single Norwegian men living in the Midwest at the time, attracted by the farming opportunities. Once she'd earned her victims' trust, she poisoned and bludgeoned them to death, and then chopped up their bodies in the cellar. Gunness measured around six-foot-tall and weighed 250 to 300 pounds, so she would have found handling her victims' bodies relatively easy.

Found in the Fire?

The day of the fire, Gunness visited an attorney, fearing for her life. She claimed her former hired hand and boyfriend, Ray Lamphere, was going to kill her, and she wanted to get her affairs in order. While Lamphere was resentful for being replaced by Gunness's new boyfriend (and final victim), Andrew Helgelien, and possibly knew about her crimes, he was only found guilty of setting the fire, not the children's murders. And the woman with the missing head has led many to doubt if Gunness died in the fire at all. Perhaps she staged the whole thing using a decoy and then disappeared without a trace.

What do policewomen Georgia Ann Robinson and Sislin Fay Allen have in common?

In 1915 a delegation of African-American women petitioned Los Angeles Police Chief Clarence Snively to hire black female officers. And in 1919, the first African-American woman was sworn into the role. Progress in the United Kingdom, however, was a bit slower.

Making History

Georgia Ann Robinson had initially joined the Los Angeles Police Department as a matron in 1916, meaning she received no pay and didn't wear a uniform. The criteria for policewomen were much higher than for the men: You had to be thirty to forty-four years of age, have a college education, be married, preferably with children, and pass a civil service exam. But the community activism worked, and on June 10, 1919, Robinson became the force's first African-American "regular policewoman," and one of the first in the country. She spent thirteen years as a police officer, working on juvenile and homicide cases.

New Hire

Forty-nine years after Robinson's swearing in ceremony, the United Kingdom got its first black female police officer. In Croydon, a nurse by the name of Sislin Fay Allen applied to a 1968 newspaper advertisement for men and women officers. At the selection day she was the only black person and one of just ten women. She took the exams and a medical, and made the cut, making history at the same time. Reporters had a field day, and she was a bit of a curiosity walking her beat. Later she was appointed to Scotland Yard's missing persons Bureau. She left the force in 1972 to move to Jamaica, where she joined the police again.

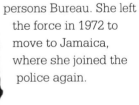

Did Lizzie Borden murder her parents?

In the late summer of 1892, the double murder of Andrew Borden and his wife Abby shocked a small Massachusetts mill town. The prime suspect was Andrew's daughter, but she was found innocent of the crime.

Ax Murderer on the Loose

It was August 4, 1892, in Fall River when thirty-two-year-old Lizzie Borden walked into the living room of the house she shared with her father, stepmother, and sister Emma. She cried out to the maid, Bridget, who came running. Lizzie's bank president father was lying dead on the sofa; his head had been struck ten or eleven times with a small sharp ax. Minutes later, they discovered Mrs. Borden upstairs, lying on the floor of the guest room. Her body was cold, and she'd been struck eighteen times by the same weapon.

Prime Suspect

Immediately, the police were suspicious of Lizzie. Her demeanor didn't live up to their expectations of how a woman should have reacted under the circumstances. She didn't show obvious signs of horror or grief in relation to the shocking sight of the bodies or the loss of her father and stepmother. And there were other factors, too. Her father was a relatively wealthy man, and the daughters stood to inherit everything. Had Lizzie murdered them for money? A drugstore clerk cast more suspicion when he revealed Lizzie had purchased the deadly poison hydrogen cyanide the day before the murders.

At the inquest, Lizzie's statements about her whereabouts and actions on the day of the murders were incomplete and sometimes contradictory. She told the police about a mysterious man who had come to the house a couple of weeks previously to do business with her father and left after an altercation, but with no name to go on, the police's minds were set: One week after the murders they charged Lizzie with the crimes. It sent shockwaves through the community. Women of her wealth and social standing were so rarely accused of any crime at all, let alone murder.

Lizzie on Trial

In the end it was this that saved her, and the fact there was no physical evidence linking her to the crime. When she went on trial ten months later, the jury just couldn't accept that a well-to-do woman could commit such a vicious and violent act—a crime for which she would have faced the death penalty (something no woman in the state had been subjected to for centuries). But the story had become a national sensation and Lizzie's reputation was in tatters. After her acquittal, she bought a large house in a rich neighborhood with her sister. Their relationship was frayed, however, and she ended up living there alone and dying in 1927, aged sixty-seven.

CRIME RHYME

Despite her name being cleared in court, a rhyme became popular that would forever paint Lizzie Borden as an evil woman who got away with murder:

Lizzie Borden took an ax
And gave her mother forty whacks
When she saw what she had done
She gave her father forty-one

Why was Miyuki Ishikawa a murderous midwife?

In the shadow of World War II, Japan was experiencing a population boom and a serious food shortage. Most people couldn't afford to have children, but abortion was illegal, and contraception was scarce. Miyuki Ishikawa found a disturbing way to "help" these desperate parents.

Duty of Carelessness

Ishikawa was a married midwife who by the late 1940s had risen up the ranks to become the director of the Kotobuki maternity hospital. While child neglect and even abandonment wasn't unheard of, Ishikawa took it to a whole new level. She was responsible for the deaths of over one hundred infants in her care through neglect. Some babies would be abandoned at the hospital intentionally, but other parents were convinced to pay Ishikawa to provide a fake death certificate and dispose of their unwanted children—a cheaper option than paying to raise a child to adulthood.

Blame the Parents

When five infant corpses were discovered in 1948, in Tokyo's Waseda district, autopsies revealed they had died of unnatural causes, and then a city-wide investigation unearthed seventy more. Ishikawa was arrested—together with her husband and a doctor—and charged with 103 deaths by omission (rather than murder), although the total death-toll could have been higher. At the time, infants had few rights under the law, and Ishikawa only received eight years for her crimes, reduced to four on appeal. It was a shocking case that led to a change in the law. Abortion was legalized in 1948 for women in specific circumstances, including those financially unable to raise a baby.

Victorian Scandal

Ishikawa's case echoed the scandalous story of Victorian nurse Amelia Dyer from the United Kingdom. Dyer had grown up in a poverty-stricken Bristol home with a mentally ill mother, and she faced more hardship as an adult when she was widowed and left with a baby to support on her own. In her desperate state, Dyer learned about the common practice of "baby farming," whereby poor women, usually single mothers, would pay a "baby farmer" to take the child off their hands. From 1869, Dyer started posting advertisements in local papers, posing as a married couple looking for a healthy child to adopt for the fee of £10. When women handed over their babies, they thought they were paying for them to go to a better life, but instead, Dyer would murder the infants by strangulation or with an opiate-laced drink.

The large number of death certificates issued for children in Dyer's care failed to raise any real red flags because of high infant mortality rates, although she did receive a six-month sentence for neglect. This didn't deter her. She continued her brutal business for nearly thirty years, traveling around England, charging women the equivalent of between £1,000 and £8,000 in today's money to take their children. She was finally caught in 1896 when a parcel containing a dead baby was found in the River Thames. Dyer's name and address were on the packaging. The number of children she killed is unknown, although estimates have put it at around 300. Unlike Ishikawa, after confessing, Dyer was hanged for her crimes in 1896.

How many "witches" were burned at the stake in Salem?

Just as the 300-year-long era of European witch hunts was dying down, leaving the tortuous deaths of tens of thousands of people, mainly women, in their wake, weird things started happening in a Massachusetts village. And witches were to blame . . .

Something Strange in the Neighborhood . . .

In January 1692 there was unrest in Salem Village (now Danvers, Massachusetts). A British–French colonial war had broken out a few years earlier, destroying parts of present-day New York, Quebec, and Nova Scotia, and sending refugees toward the Massachusetts Bay region. The population rise led to food shortages and coincided with a smallpox epidemic. Plus, there were tensions with indigenous tribes and the village's more affluent neighbor, Salem Town. It was amidst this melting pot of conflict, Puritanical beliefs, and xenophobia that a number of local girls started to show some unusual symptoms.

First Elizabeth Parris, nine, and Abigail Williams, eleven, daughter and niece of Salem Village's first ordained minister, Samuel Parris, started having fits and erupting into violent outbursts. The doctor blamed the devil, and shortly after other girls came down with the same symptoms. They were interviewed by magistrates, and under pressure, the young girls blamed their afflictions on three women: Sarah Good, a local beggar; Tituba, the Parris's Caribbean slave; and Sarah Osborne, an elderly lady living in poverty. In March the accused women were interrogated. It lasted for days, and while Osborne and Good denied the charges, Tituba confessed that she was doing the devil's work and there were others just like her. All three were sent to prison. But they weren't the last.

Hung for Heresy

Known as the Salem Witch Trials, what followed was a period of suspicion, accusation, and execution that lasted for months. On May 27 a special court was established to deal with the number of witchcraft cases. Bridget Bishop was the first woman hanged on June 10, and she was followed to the gallows by eighteen others. One man was killed by being pressed to death with stones, and seven people died in jail. Around 200 women, men, and children spent time in prison accused of practicing the devil's magic. But nobody was burnt at the stake. The hysteria soon died down and the court was disbanded in October. The following May, Governor William Phipps pardoned all those who stood charged with witchcraft. In 1711 a bill was passed to restore the accused people's rights and good names, with £600 in restitution paid to their heirs. It was too little, too late.

FUNGAL INFECTION?

If there was something fishy going on in Salem Village in 1692, trust science to have come up with a theory as to what. While numerous studies and suggestions have been made over the years, Linnda R. Caporael's 1976 paper, "Ergotism: The Satan Loosed in Salem," published in Science, said the girls' muscle spasms and delusions could have been a result of eating rye or wheat contaminated by a fungus called ergot. It grows in the warm, damp climate typical of the marshes that would have been found in Salem Village and is known to cause medical symptoms like vomiting, shaking, and hallucinations.

Who caught the taxi cab robbers?

In 1912 Isabella Goodwin was a police detective in all but name, until she solved a crime that had baffled New York Police Department's (NYPD'S) finest for weeks.

Matronly Duties

After working as a police station matron for six years, taking care of female suspects and witnesses, Goodwin was asked to go undercover to bring down an illegal gambling den. Her appearance worked to her advantage—no one suspected an attractive, middle-aged woman to be doing the police's dirty work. After successfully gathering evidence that helped bring down the crooks, she was sent on more assignments, investigating illegal fortune-tellers and phony doctors, and testifying in court to help convict them. Despite her success, she didn't have the arresting powers or salary of a police officer.

Most Wanted

On February 15, 1912, two bank employees were taking a taxi to transfer cash from one bank to another when three men robbed them of $25,000 and took off. With sixty detectives on the case, the NYPD identified the lead suspects, but their whereabouts were unknown. With the case going cold, Goodwin was sent undercover as a cleaner at one of the suspects' girlfriend's home. She discovered that the woman and her criminal beau were planning their escape by train to San Francisco. This was the key evidence police needed, and they picked the pair up at Grand Central Station's ticket booth. The robber soon turned on his accomplices, and the case was cracked. Goodwin's actions got her promoted, making her the NYPD's first female detective.

CRIME AND PUNISHMENT

You've seen all the evidence and followed all the leads. Now it's time for a punishing quiz that will test your clue-cracking capabilities to the max.

Questions

1. In which American city did assassins plan to murder President-elect Abraham Lincoln as he changed trains on his way to the capital?

2. From which region did most of Belle Gunness's victims come from?

3. What does modern science think might have caused the symptoms exhibited by girls in Salem Village in 1672?

4. Who was the LAPD's first African-American police officer?

5. What was a ducking stool?

6. In Victorian England, what was "baby farming"?

7. Whose Wild West touring show did Annie Oakley appear in?

8. Before she was an NYPD detective, what was Isabella Goodwin's job title?

9. What were the peasant laborers of feudal Russia known as?

10. What weapon was Lizzie Borden accused of using to kill her father and stepmother?

Turn to page 216 for the answers.

WHICH "LITTLE WOMAN" WROTE A BOOK THAT STARTED A WAR?

HOW DID A BOOK GALVANIZE A WORLDWIDE ENVIRONMENTAL MOVEMENT?

HOW DID ARTEMISIA GENTILESCHI SUFFER FOR HER ART?

HOW MANY VERSIONS ARE THERE OF ANNE FRANK'S DIARY?

ARTS AND LITERATURE

WHICH FAMOUS SCULPTURE WAS LOST IN A CHICAGO SUBURB?

WHO WROTE THE WORLD'S FIRST NOVEL?

Who wrote the world's first novel?

The Tale of Genji is widely considered to be the world's first modern novel, published in the early eleventh century in Japan. Its author was Murasaki Shikibu, an aristocrat who went on to become a lady-in-waiting and tutor to Empress Shōshi.

Sheltered and Scholarly

As a female member of the aristocracy, Shikibu lived a sheltered life. She was rarely seen in public, and when she was she would be behind a screen or curtain, as was customary then. She was the daughter of a minor official and scholar named Fujiwara no Tametoki,

and her great-grandfather and grandfather had been members of the Heian elite and respected poets. She accompanied her father as he served as provincial governor in Harima, Echigo, and Echizen.

Shikibu was highly educated and considered somewhat of a literary prodigy. She was also proficient in Chinese and its literature, which at the time was exclusively used by Japanese men—her diaries suggest she learned it by listening at the door when her father was teaching her brother. Around AD 998 she married Fujiwara no Nobutaka, a second cousin who was much older than her, and gave birth to a daughter, Kenshi. A couple of years later, however, her husband died, and rather than remarry, the widowed Shikibu started work on a book, *The Tale of Genji*.

The First of its Kind

Believed to have been written between 1001 and 1010 (scholars differ on the precise dates), the fifty-four-chapter book centers around the life of Prince Genji—the son of an emperor who is reduced to the status of a commoner for political reasons. The story follows

Shikibu lived at a time when Japanese women's real names weren't recorded. They might be referred to by a nickname that often related to the rank of a father or husband. "Shikibu" means "Bureau of Ceremonial" and refers to a post her father once held. "Murasaki" is the Japanese word for the color purple or lavender, as well as a plant that produces purple dye. It's also the name of the main female character in *The Tale of Genji*.

Essential Reading

Shikibu's book not only helped propel her up the social order during her lifetime, it soon became essential reading for the Japanese upper classes. By the late twelfth century it was required reading for scholars and poets. But it was only with the arrival of the printing press in the seventeenth century that Shikibu's work finally became available to the masses. The book is an intrinsic part of contemporary Japanese culture, with high schools regularly teaching parts of it in classical Japanese and a number of more modern translations available. More than two million copies have been sold since sale records began to be tracked.

" . . . the fifty-four-chapter book centers around the life of Prince Genji . . . "

his romantic conquests and is a detailed portrayal of aristocratic life of the period but also gives a rare insight into the lives of these cloistered women, through carefully delineated characters. Unlike other writings from the period that simply recorded events or invented a story, Shikibu's book was a work of art with complex human insight.

Which famous sculpture was lost in a Chicago suburb?

As the world's first African-American sculptor, Edmonia Lewis was used to standing out from the crowd. But the artwork she made for the Centennial Exhibition in Philadelphia divided her contemporaries.

Morbid Marble

The exhibition, which marked the hundred-year anniversary of the signing of the U.S. Declaration of Independence, took place in 1876. Lewis's *The Death of Cleopatra* was a 3,000-pound marble marvel. It depicted the Egyptian queen Cleopatra after she had chosen suicide by poison rather than surrender to Roman invaders. The historical scene was a popular one among sculptors of the period, but typically Cleopatra was shown contemplating suicide, whereas Lewis's queen was already deceased, with a bare breast to boot. While some regarded the realistic sculpture as "ghastly," it was deemed the most impressive work at the exhibition.

Missing at the Mall

After the exhibition ended, the highly acclaimed work was lost for nearly a century. There were reports of it being on display at a saloon in 1892, and then it spent some time at Harlem Race Track in a suburb of Chicago, but when the venue closed, the sculpture remained there. Over the years, the site was first a golf course, then a munitions factory, and then a bulk mail center. In the 1980s, after *Cleopatra* had been salvaged by a fire inspector and some eager Boy Scouts, who covered her in white and purple house paint, she was discovered by an independent curator and Lewis biographer and rescued from a life of obscurity. Since 1994 the sculpture has been part of the Smithsonian's permanent collection.

Who was Edmonia Lewis?

The daughter of a Chippewa mother and African-American father, Lewis was orphaned at a young age and raised by her nomadic maternal aunts in upstate New York. A wealthy half-brother helped to pay for her education, however, and she attended Oberlin College in Ohio in 1859. Although Oberlin officially accepted women and African-American students, Lewis faced discrimination there. She was abducted, assaulted, and left for dead by white extremists after she was accused of poisoning two white women. She persevered until the following year, when she was accused of stealing art supplies and was refused entry to the final semester of her education, meaning she never graduated.

After a brief stint in Boston, where she received some formal training from the sculptor Edward A. Brackett, she made the decision to go to Europe—she funded the trip by selling busts of celebrated abolitionists. Setting sail in 1859, she traveled to London, Paris, Florence, and Rome, where she rented a studio and settled into Italian life among her contemporaries. There were plenty of other female American sculptors working there too, including Emma Stebbins, Margaret Foley, and Harriet Goodhue Hosmer. Like most artists of the time, Lewis made a living producing trend-led works people wanted to buy and traveling back and forth across the Atlantic to sell them and earn commissions. Americans such as Frederick Douglass and Ulysses S. Grant visited her studio and sat for her while traveling the Grand Tour of Europe. She sculpted religious subjects, Native Americans, mythical scenes, and her patrons. Her works sold for thousands of dollars.

How did a book galvanize a worldwide environmental movement?

The world's most powerful pesticide was made available for civilian use in 1945. Dichlorodiphenyltrichloroethane (DDT) was capable of wiping out hundreds of different insects at once. Most people didn't give it a second thought; farmers and home-growers were simply grateful for the advantages it offered them over nature. Then there was Rachel Carson . . .

A Life Aquatic

Carson was a nature-lover from childhood, growing up on a farm in Pennsylvania. She took her studies seriously, attending Pennsylvania College for Women, Woods Hole Oceanographic Institute, and Johns Hopkins University, where she received a master's degree in zoology in 1932. She aced the civil service exam to become only the second woman hired by the U.S. Bureau of Fisheries, where she spent fifteen years working as a marine biologist, writing about science for the public. It was during this time that she also wrote her own books about aquatic life, including *The Sea Around Us* and *The Edge of the Sea*, which was an international bestseller.

Disaster Looming

In 1958, now a respected and published authority, Carson turned her attention to the dangers of DDT. It was developed in 1939 and its inventor, Paul Hermann Müller, was awarded the Nobel Prize in Physiology or Medicine. The insecticide was widely used during World War II to prevent malaria and typhus infection of U.S. troops and had become a popular home remedy for killing house flies and fogging for mosquitoes. Carson received a letter from a friend in Massachusetts who was concerned about the number of birds that had died in the area as a result of these mass sprayings. Despite her status as a best-selling author, Carson was unable to convince magazine editors to publish a story about the potentially catastrophic effects of the chemical. Her views were controversial, and no one wanted to hear them. So she wrote a book.

Silent no More

After four years of painstaking research, Carson published *Silent Spring* in 1962. The book chronicled the passage of DDT through the food chain, and laid bare the potential genetic damage and disease, particularly cancer, that its use could cause in humans. It spoke of the compound's long-lasting toxicity and the contamination of the food supply. The book had an immediate impact, opening the public consciousness to environmental damage and the importance of industry regulation. The research was accompanied by fifty-five pages of notes and was approved by numerous experts and eminent scientists. If the chemical industry had any ammunition against Carson, it was petty and personal.

Things changed very quickly. President John F. Kennedy ordered the President's Science Advisory Committee to look into the issues surrounding DDT, and the outcry sparked a movement of environmentalism and anti-pesticide sentiment that led to the creation of the U.S. Environmental Protection Agency in 1970. The U.S. Court of Appeals upheld a ban on DDT in 1973. Sadly, Carson wouldn't live to see it. When she appeared on TV in a CBS special in 1963, 15 million viewers tuned in to watch her discuss the issues in the book. A year later she died of breast cancer.

How did Artemisia Gentileschi suffer for her art?

Artemisia Gentileschi was a rare thing: a successful female painter during the Italian Baroque period. But despite her success, one horrific incident changed her life forever and no doubt had a huge influence on the work she produced.

Art Imitates Life

In Gentileschi's painting *Judith Slaying Holofernes* the Old Testament story of the Israelites' enemy having his head cut off by a female assassin is depicted with stark brutality. Judith, with the help of a servant girl, pins Holofernes to the bed and saws through his neck with a sword. It's painted in the style of her father's friend, Caravaggio— one of the late sixteenth-century's most successful and convention-defying painters. But like many of Gentileschi's paintings, the work could also be considered a self-portrait, a fantastical retelling of her rage toward the man who raped her when she was a teenager.

Artistic Upbringing

Gentileschi was born in 1593 in Rome. Her father was a painter whose studio was filled with realist works and painting experiments. While she grew up surrounded by a vibrant artistic culture, Gentileschi was not an aristocrat, so marriage and motherhood or a life in a nunnery would have been the most likely routes for her. Instead, she became her father's assistant, learning the skills and developing her incredible talent. Eventually her father consented to her chosen path and took to promoting her work. He even hired a popular painter named Agostino Tassi to help further her painting skills.

Reputation on Trial

In 1612 Gentileschi's father accused Tassi of raping his daughter. According to the surviving court transcripts, Tassi had made increasingly menacing advances toward the young woman before finally attacking her in her own home. An unmarried woman's reputation was everything, so not only did Gentileschi have to deal with the inner turmoil of this violent attack, she also had to face a humiliating seven-month-long public trial. It was the talk of Rome, and Tassi's reputation was destroyed as witness after witness testified to his bad character (there was even a claim he had killed his own wife). Not that it mattered. While the court found him guilty, Tassi was a favorite painter of the Pope, and he was released prematurely from his prison sentence. Gentileschi's name would always be associated with the rape case, but her reputation was restored enough to secure a marriage and continue her career. She went on to make works for King Charles I of England and the Medici family.

A TORTURED VICTIM

Not only did Gentileschi have to undergo a gynecological examination to prove her claims, she was also subject to the *sibille* or thumbscrews—a form of torture where ropes are progressively tightened around the fingers or thumbs. Later devices of this nature were steel contraptions, some containing spikes. The excruciating pain was supposed to make sure the witness was being truthful, but these devices were also used to torture criminals. As the cords around Gentileschi's fingers tightened, the transcripts reveal she cried out, "It is true, it is true, it is true!"

Why was Edith Wharton's Pulitzer Prize win bittersweet?

In 1921, the Pulitzer Prizes were just four years old, but a woman had yet to win one. Then Edith Wharton published *The Age of Innocence* and the "novel" prize was hers.

> "When I discovered that I was being rewarded . . . for uplifting American morals, I confess I did despair."

Nod to Novels

The Pulitzer Prizes were specified in the will of Joseph Pulitzer. In the latter part of the nineteenth century he stood out as America's most skillful of publishers, whose efforts and determination helped shaped the newspaper industry today. The first prizes, administered by Columbia University, were doled out in 1917, and included accolades for journalism, letters and drama, and education. The novel prize (later the fiction prize) was "for the American novel published during the year which shall best present the whole atmosphere of American life, and the highest stand of American manners and manhood." Wharton's book, the author's twelfth, was about New York high society during the 1870s. But it almost didn't win.

A Close Call

Before the award recipients were formally announced, one of the prize's jurors, Robert Morss Lovett, wrote in *The New Republic*, of which he was associate editor, that Wharton's book hadn't been the jury's first choice. They preferred Sinclair Lewis's *Main Street*, a best-selling small-town satire. But the board had overturned their decision. When Lewis found out he hadn't won, he wrote to Wharton to congratulate her. Her reply: "When I discovered that I was being rewarded . . . for uplifting American morals, I confess I did despair. Subsequently, when I found the prize should really have been yours . . . disgust was added to despair."

Why did Frida Kahlo lie about her age?

Of the fifty-five paintings Frida Kahlo created, one third of them were of herself. These self-portraits were often emotive works that evoked her personal struggles: heartbreak, her physical health, and miscarriage. She might have painted her own reality, but she was far from vain. So why did she tell reporters she was three years younger than she was?

Proud to be Mexican

Kahlo claimed she was born in 1910, instead of 1907, her actual birth year. But it had more to do with patriotism than preserving a youthful image. The year 1910 was also the year the Mexican Revolution began, and it marked the overthrow of President Porfirio Díaz. Kahlo traveled all over the world, living in San Francisco, New York, and Paris, but it was Mexico City where she felt she truly belonged. In the years since her death, Kahlo has become a fierce feminist and socialist icon. She was a member of the Mexican Communist Party and was a central figure in the "Mexicanidad" movement, a resurgence and celebration of indigenous Mexican culture.

Cultural Clothes

In Kahlo's paintings she incorporated her mixed-ancestry heritage, including Aztec symbols, skulls, flowers, and monkeys, as well as the religious iconography of *retablos* (altar paintings) or *ex-votos* (tin paintings offered in prayer). And that admiration for her heritage extended through to her fashion, too. The *huipile* (blouse) and long colorful *falta* (skirt) combo she is so well recognized for today came from the region's Tehuantepec people—a matriarchal society known for its female leadership.

Which "little woman" wrote a book that started a war?

It was the best-selling novel of the nineteenth century, selling over 300,000 copies in the United States in its first year alone, but did Harriet Beecher Stowe's *Uncle Tom's Cabin* actually start the American Civil War?

The Greatest Book of Its Kind

Born into a prominent social-reformist Connecticut family, Stowe was a staunch abolitionist. She was heavily influenced by her experiences meeting runaway slaves while living in Ohio, which was on the border with Kentucky, a slave state, and the tragic death of her eighteen-month-old son—many slave mothers had their babies stolen and sold. After the passing of the Fugitive Slave Act of 1850, which made it illegal for antislavery citizens in the North to harbor or help escaped slaves, Stowe started writing *Uncle Tom's Cabin*.

Published in 1852, the story centers around Tom, an honorable slave who is taken from his family and sold at auction. It follows his travels on a slave ship, where he saves the life of a white girl—they become friends—then on the plantation where he helps another slave, Eliza, escape with her son. He is eventually beaten to death. The book's unique depictions of African-Americans and its damning portrayal of the slave trade made it

hugely controversial in the South, where it was banned in some states. In the North it fueled the antislavery movement and popularity for the Republican Party. This ultimately led to President Abraham Lincoln winning the election in 1860 and the public support for the Civil War which followed.

Lincoln Legacy

In November 1862, eighteen months into the Civil War, Stowe traveled to Washington, DC, to meet the president. While Lincoln was against the spread of slavery into states where it no longer existed, only a few months earlier he had written that if it was possible to save the Union without eradicating slavery, he would do it. His goal was unification. But what he didn't want was an uprising from within his own party or foreign intervention in the war, so in September 1862 he issued a warning to the Confederate states: rejoin the Union by January 1, 1863, or he would issue the Emancipation Proclamation, changing the legal status of the South's 3.5 million slaves to free people.

One of the most famous women in America, Stowe was writing an article for a British women's magazine to drum up support for the Union. She argued that, as far as the North was concerned, the whole reason for the war was to end slavery. When Stowe met Lincoln, she wanted to find out how seriously the Proclamation would be taken, and if he was committed to abolition. The legend goes that when they met, he said to her: "So you're the little woman who wrote the book that made this great war!" Lincoln's motivations for the war were political and economic, but whether he said these words or not, it's likely he acknowledged the importance abolitionists like Stowe, and her book, played in winning the hearts and minds of the people.

Who were the forgotten women of the Bauhaus?

When Walter Gropius founded the Bauhaus School in Weimar, Germany in 1919, more women than men applied to take its art and design courses. But theirs weren't the most famous names that emerged from its walls.

A New Kind of School

German women had only previously been able to receive an artistic education from home tutors, but the Bauhaus was a new kind of art school based on the principle of Gesamtkunstwerk—a nonhierarchical fusion of art, architecture, and design. It also declared equality between the sexes. In the school's manifesto it said that "any person of good repute" was welcome to attend "without regard to age or sex." But the sexist attitudes of the day still prevailed. Walter Gropius insisted that there would be "no difference between the beautiful and the strong sex," this very distinction revealing how women would be sidelined and shoehorned into particular practices.

Division of Labor

From the start, the men were tutored in painting and carving. Meanwhile, the women were encouraged to pursue weaving. While the work produced was radical, Gropius was keen to keep women working on two-dimensional projects, believing that only men could handle three dimensions, and fearful of the school's professional reputation being tarnished by women's involvement. He even set a limit on the number of women who could be admitted. By the time the school closed in 1933, under pressure from the Nazi regime, it had become centered around architecture and metal works, both fields from which women had been barred.

Women of the Bauhaus

Names like Gropius, Klee, Kandinsky, and Mies van der Rohe are ubiquitous with fine art, architecture, and design, but who were the Bauhaus women who studied alongside them?

GUNTA STÖLZL headed up the weaving workshop for five years. In the years after she ran her own successful weaving business—her works were acquired by Museum of Modern Art in New York and the Victoria and Albert Museum in London.

BENITA KOCH-OTTE was a high-school drawing and handicraft teacher when she joined the Bauhaus. Later in life she became director of a textile mill—her fabrics are still produced today.

MARGUERITE FRIEDLAENDER-WILDENHAIN and **MARGARETE HEYMANN** both found success with ceramics, the former with America's Pond Hall pottery, and the latter both in Germany with Haël-Werkstätten and then in England with Greta pottery.

ALMA SIEDHOFF-BUSCHER was part of the wood-sculpture department, at Bauhaus, which was rare for a woman. She was a toy and furniture designer, known for her ship-building block game, cut-out kits, and her modular children's room furniture. She died in a bombing raid in 1944.

ANNI ALBERS took over the weaving workshop from Stölzl and became an innovative textile designer. She fled Nazi Germany for North Carolina in 1933 where she taught at the experimental Black Mountain College art school. She was the first designer to have a solo show at New York's Museum of Modern Art.

MARIANNE BRANDT was the first woman to be admitted to the Bauhaus's metalwork department (and the first to run it in 1928). She became famous for her iconic 1920 Kandem bedside lamp and coffee sets.

How many versions are there of Anne Frank's diary?

Published for the first time in 1947, and since translated into more than seventy languages, Anne Frank's wartime diary is one of the most famous books of its kind, but what is less well known is that she wrote two versions of it.

A Young Diarist

On her thirteenth birthday on June 12, 1942, in Amsterdam, Netherlands, Frank received a red and white checkered diary as a present. Less than a month later, fearing for their lives as the Nazi occupiers' anti-Semitic policies became more troubling, her family went into hiding in a secret annex at the back of her father's office building. For the next two years,

Anne continued to write in her diary (it spanned three further notebooks), but these were her private musings, not intended for others. Then, in the spring of 1944, she heard a request on the radio from the exiled Dutch government for eyewitness accounts of people suffering under occupation, and she started to rewrite her diary with the hope of publishing it after the war. This second version filled 215 loose pages.

Frank wrote at length about her confined living quarters and daily routine, her family and fellow residents-in-hiding, her dreams for the future, as well as more complex thoughts and ideas about her burgeoning adulthood, Jewish faith,

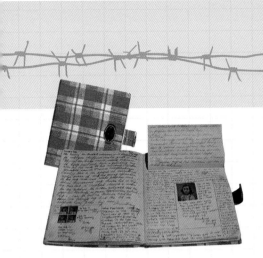

and her longing for the freedom of nature. During the two years of writing, Frank found comfort and support in her diary, and a real passion for writing. As well as her personal thoughts, she wrote about books she enjoyed and even authored her own short stories. Her wish was to become a famous writer after the war.

His Daughter's Legacy

Frank continued to write her diary until just a few days before the family were caught on August 4, 1944, and sent to Auschwitz. She died of typhus in the winter of 1945 at Bergen-Belsen concentration camp. Two of the Dutch helpers, Miep Gies and Bep Voskuijl, who risked their lives for the Franks, gathered up Anne's writings and kept them safe. After the war, they gave

THE CRITICAL EDITION

In 1986 a Dutch critical edition of the diary was published, which included both versions in parallel, giving readers an insight into Frank's self-editing process. It had been unraveled by the Netherlands Institute for War Documentation, which had commissioned a forensic study of the manuscripts after Otto Frank died in 1980. There was some speculation as to whether Otto had written some of the diary himself, but the research proved definitively that the handwriting was Anne's and the paper, ink, and glue used were the type found in Amsterdam when she was writing. It was published in three volumes, totaling 714 pages.

them to her father, Otto Frank—the only member of the family to survive. From the two versions, Otto compiled a third version, which became the original published book, *The Diary of a Young Girl*.

Why did a performance artist walk for 1,550 miles?

Often referred to as the "Grandmother of Performance Art," Marina Abramović became famous in the 1970s for her artistic feats of endurance. In 1976 she met German performance artist Ulay, and the two began a twelve-year relationship and professional collaboration.

Artists in Love

Their notorious performances included "Relation in Time," where they sat back to back with their hair tied together for seventeen hours, and "Breathing In/Breathing Out," where they breathed in and out of each other's mouths for twenty minutes, to the point of near-suffocation. Their final collaboration in 1988 was called "Lovers: The Great Wall of China Walk." When they started negotiating with Chinese authorities to walk from different ends of the Great Wall of China to meet in the middle, they'd planned to marry when they finished. But by the time permission came, their relationship was on the rocks and they decided to make it their last hurrah.

The Final Performance

Abramović set off from the eastern end by the Yellow Sea, while Ulay started in the west on the edge of the Gobi Desert. They both walked around 1,550 miles over ninety days and were reunited at Er Lang Shan in Shaanxi province. There they said their goodbyes. In 2010 they were reunited for the first time in over twenty years when Abramović was performing "The Artist Is Present" at the MoMA gallery in New York. Over 736 hours, she sat in the museum's atrium while spectators queued up to sit opposite her. Much to her surprise, one of them was Ulay.

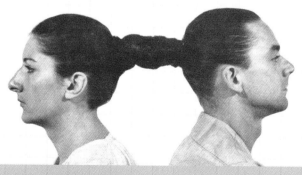

ARTS AND LITERATURE

From paintbrushes to typewriters, these women wielded their artistic tools to great effect. Now it's time for you to make a masterpiece of the mind with this quiz.

Questions

1. Why was Artemisia Gentileschi subjected to torture at her rapist's trial?
2. *Silent Spring* looked into the harmful effects of which insecticide?
3. Why did Anne Frank rewrite her diary?
4. Which patriotic year did Frida Kahlo claim she was born in?
5. What was different about Edmonia Lewis's *The Death of Cleopatra* sculpture?
6. What is the name of the first modern novel, written by Murasaki Shikibu?
7. What were women encouraged to pursue at the Bauhaus?
8. What is the name of the titular character in Harriet Beecher Stowe's nineteenth-century bestseller?
9. How far did Marina Abramović walk in "Lovers: The Great Wall of China Walk" before ending her relationship with Ulay—15 miles, 150 miles, or 1,550 miles?
10. What was Edith Wharton the first woman to win?

Turn to page 216 for the answers.

HOW DID A NOVICE NUN REVOLUTIONIZE THE CIRCUS?

WHAT DID ANNA PAVLOVA ASK FOR ON HER DEATHBED?

WHY DID EDITH PIAF POSE FOR PHOTOS WITH FRENCH POWS?

WHO WERE THE FIRST WOMEN TO PERFORM ON THE LONDON STAGE?

WHAT DID THE "EUROPEAN QUEEN OF PIANO" DO AGAINST HER FATHER'S WILL?

SHOW BUSINESS

WHAT COULDN'T FILM STAR ANNA MAY WONG DO ON SCREEN?

WHICH FAMOUS FAN HELPED ELLA FITZGERALD GET HER CAREER OFF THE GROUND?

What couldn't film star Anna May Wong do on screen?

Anna May Wong rose to fame in the early days of Hollywood cinema, but strict censorship codes prevented the Chinese-American actress from pursuing meaty roles and falling in love on screen.

Cinematic Code of Conduct

Drawn up in the 1930s, the Motion Picture Production Code, popularly known as the Hays Code, laid out what was acceptable on screen in Hollywood movies. From bad language and nudity to drug trafficking and scenes of childbirth, it ruled out a lot. One pervasive taboo that it took a long time for the industry to shake was the ban on miscegenation (marital or sexual relations between different races). Californian-born Wong didn't let industry prejudice put her off, and

she won her first lead role in the silent film *The Toll of the Sea* in 1922. It was a hit, and Wong was soon starring opposite Douglas Fairbanks in *The Thief of Baghdad*, playing a seductive temptress—a role she would continue to fill for much of her career.

A Star in Europe

In 1927, Wong traveled to Europe, where she hoped to avoid such stringent typecasting and the restraints of Hollywood's segregated social scene. Capitalizing on her stardom, she made *Pavement Butterfly* and *Piccadilly*, among others—films that cemented

her reputation as an actress. But even in the United Kingdom the British Board of Film Censors' ban on "parti-colored kissing" meant she never got to kiss a white costar on screen, even when their characters fell in love.

A few years later in hit "talkies" like *Daughter of the Dragon* and *Shanghai Express*, she was relegated to "exotic" best friend or "dragon lady" racial stereotypes. More substantial Chinese characters were often played by white women, most notably in the 1930 adaptation of Pearl S. Buck's Pulitzer-Prize-winning novel *The Good Earth*, about a Chinese family saga set in the lead-up to World War I. Wong had openly expressed interest in the lead role, but when the male lead went to a white Austrian actor, there was no question in the studio's mind that the woman cast opposite him would be white. They cast German-born Luise Rainer, who won the 1937 Best Actress Oscar for her "yellowface" portrayal.

Final Frustrations

In 1930, frustrated with the parts on offer, Wong told an Australian newspaper: "I can't for the life of me understand why a white man couldn't fall in love with me on the screen . . . If it were possible to overcome this terrible censorship barrier, a new field would open for me." Unfortunately, by the end of the 1930s, and with no alluring prospects, Wong's star-power started to fade. However, she did have her own TV show, *The Gallery of Madame Liu-Tsong*, in 1951, making her the first Asian-American star to do so. As competition from television and foreign films increased, the code faced more and more pushback from filmmakers. In the late 1960s it was abandoned altogether.

The first interracial kiss on the big screen appeared in 1957's *Island in the Sun*, only a few years before Wong died of a heart attack in 1961.

Why did Edith Piaf pose for photos with French POWs?

When French singer Edith Piaf died in 1963, she received her country's highest honor—the tricolor flag was draped over her coffin and her funeral procession drew tens of thousands of mourners to the streets, bringing Paris to a standstill. She was a musical legend, but more than that, her wartime efforts saved lives.

Je Ne Regrette Rien

When the Nazis occupied France in 1940, Piaf was a twenty-five-year-old singing sensation. Discovered on the streets of Paris's red-light district five years earlier, the 4-foot-10-inch performer had already lived through a troubled upbringing—she'd grown up in a bordello, been briefly blinded as a child, and had battled alcoholism. When she was asked to sing for German soldiers by the Nazis, she insisted that French prisoners be allowed to watch her performances, too. As she toured the prison camps, she smuggled maps and compasses to her fellow countrymen. Then, at Stalag III-D camp near Berlin, she insisted on having her photograph taken with all the inmates. The photos were then delivered to her influential friends, who used them to make ID papers for the prisoners, declaring them to be free French workers living in Germany. When she revisited the camp for a second performance, she delivered their new documents, enabling up to 300 people to escape.

Piaf wrote many of her own songs, including the renowned "La Vie En Rose." After the war she went on to have great success, especially in America, where she played Carnegie Hall twice and helped to popularize the French language.

Who was known as a "female Shakespeare"?

Joanna Baillie earned herself comparisons to Shakespeare in her own lifetime, but today her name is a lot less well-known. Who was the Scottish poet and playwright?

Poetic Origins

Baillie was born in 1762 in Bothwell, Scotland, and could trace her ancestral line back to Sir William Wallace, but she soon found fame for herself. She came from an intellectual family, who were part of the Scottish Enlightenment, and she started writing poetry when she was just eleven years old. Despite being warned off poetry by her mother, she continued to write it along with drama and songs, working in both English and Scots. Her uncle was celebrated physician and anatomist William Hunter. On his death, her brother inherited his London home and School of Anatomy, and so in 1783 she moved to England to keep house for him.

The London Literati

It was here that she mixed with the brightest literary lights of the day—William Wordsworth, Lord Byron, Anna Letitia Barbauld, and Sir Walter Scott—and embarked on her most ambitious project: A three-volume collection titled *Plays on the Passions*. Published between 1798 and 1812, the series of comedies and tragedies covers themes of love, hatred, and jealousy. Initially, she kept her identity a secret—it was more common for women to write closet plays (to be read rather than performed), but hers were intended for the stage. Throughout her life she published twenty-seven plays, successful collections of poetry, including *Fugitive Verses*, and lyrics that were set to music by Beethoven and Haydn.

Which famous fan helped Ella Fitzgerald get her career off the ground?

QUESTION 97

Ella Fitzgerald got her first big break when she wowed the crowds at New York's Apollo Theater in 1934. It was amateur night, and she'd entered the competition as a dancer. But when she saw the stiff competition backstage, she decided to switch to singing instead. Just as well: She bagged the $25 prize, plotting the first point on a trajectory to superstardom. But it was an unlikely friendship with another big name that helped her kick things up a notch.

The Hot Ticket in Town

Opened in 1941, the Mocambo nightclub on Los Angeles' famous Sunset Strip was the place to be and be seen in the 1950s. The club was renowned for putting on the best of the best and helping to make the careers of leading jazz artists of the era. In 1943, when Frank Sinatra left the Tommy Dorsey Orchestra, he chose the Mocambo as the place to launch his solo career, to much aplomb. In an era when segregation was still rife, owner Charlie Morrison put on some of the best African-American artists— Eartha Kitt, Herb Jeffries, and Joyce Bryant all performed there. But up-and-coming New Yorker Ella Fitzgerald was having trouble booking a gig. Not because of her race, but because she wasn't considered glamorous enough.

Famous Friend

In 1972, Fitzgerald gave an interview where she revealed that it was Hollywood starlet Marilyn Monroe who got her the gig. Monroe was a huge fan— she'd been introduced to Fitzgerald's music by her vocal coach. The two women were pictured together when Fitzgerald played another Hollywood jazz venue, the Tiffany Club, in 1954. Monroe was also a frequent visitor to the Mocambo, so when she heard Fitzgerald hadn't played there, she personally petitioned Morrison to book the singer, promising to sit on the front row every night she performed. The publicity Monroe brought with her wherever she went was too much for the nightclub owner to resist, and Fitzgerald played a ten-night run at the Mocambo in March 1955.

The Mocambo closed two years later, but because of Marilyn's support, Fitzgerald said: "I never had to play a small jazz club again." Fitzgerald's career went from strength to strength. In 1958, she became the first African-American woman to win a Grammy Award. In the ten years after her first Mocambo appearance, she recorded a nineteen-volume series of songbooks, including nearly 250 songs. She remains one of the best-selling jazz vocalists in history.

MUSICAL MONROE

Monroe's vocal coach for the film *Gentlemen Prefer Blondes* said, "Marilyn had a problem with singing in tune, but everything else she did was wonderful." Not that this mattered—one of Monroe's most famous moments came in 1962, a few months before her death, when she sang "Happy Birthday" to President John F. Kennedy at Madison Square Garden in New York City. The event was a Democratic Party super fundraiser, and Monroe stole the show. The iconic sequined dress she wore for the performance sold at auction in 2016 for $4.8 million.

Did Yoko Ono break up the Beatles?

In 2012, Sir Paul McCartney gave an in-depth interview with David Frost. It was forty-two years since the official break-up of the Beatles and he was categorical in his recollection of how it went down. "She certainly didn't break the group up," he said of John Lennon's wife, Yoko Ono.

End of An Era

For decades the Japanese artist and musician was blamed by die-hard fans for the band's decline, but McCartney said it had far more to do with the death of the band's manager Brian Epstein and his replacement Allen Klein, than with Ono. He said Klein created a rift between McCartney and the others, causing them to fight among themselves and eventually call it quits. The Liverpudlian musician even credited Ono with inspiring some of Lennon's greatest hits, including

"Imagine." "I don't think he would have done that without Yoko," McCartney said, "so I don't think you can blame her for anything."

But blame her they did. Ono was vilified as a "Japanese witch" who had seduced an unwitting Lennon and kept him away from the band. Her own talents were disregarded at best and ridiculed at worst. She was unable to shake the unveiled racism and misogyny, even after Lennon was shot dead outside the New York home they shared in 1980. It probably didn't help matters that Lennon had made clear his devotion to Ono and how meeting her had unconsciously led to him taking a step away from the other Beatles members. "The old gang of mine was over the moment I met her," Lennon said in a 1980 interview with *Playboy* magazine, which hit newsstands two days before his death. "I didn't consciously know it at the time, but that's what was going on. As soon as I met her, that was the end of the boys."

Ono the Artist

Raised in Tokyo by wealthy conservative parents, Ono found solace in music and art. After her family emigrated to New York, she attended a liberal arts college there and immersed herself in the radical politics of the 1950s. She socialized with avant-garde composers John Cage and Toshi Ichiyanagi (the latter became her first husband). In Manhattan she pursued her own artistic career. She was a member of the Fluxus art group, and curated some of the 1960s "happenings"—experimental performances combining dance, theater, music, and visual art—in her downtown loft space, earning herself the title "High Priestess of the Happening." She made art films and in 1964 published *Grapefruit*, a book of performance poetry. One of her most famous works was 1966's "Cut Piece," in which she sat in a theater and invited the audience to cut up her clothes with scissors.

IN BED WITH JOHN

It was while putting on a solo show at the Indica Gallery in London that she met John Lennon. Together they would go on to collaborate on a number of projects, most famously their two 1969 "Bed-ins," where they invited the press into hotel suites, in Amsterdam and Montreal, and used the publicity surrounding their marriage to promote world peace during the Vietnam War.

What did the "European Queen of Piano" do against her father's will?

Clara Schumann's father raised her to be what he was not—a concert pianist of the highest caliber—whether she wanted to or not. But when it came to matters of the heart, he was powerless to prevent her from following hers.

The Prodigious Daughter

Born Clara Wieck in 1819, her father was Friedrich Wieck, a well-connected piano teacher who tutored her from the age of five. Wieck supervised her formal training in theory and composition. By the time she was nine, she was ready for her first public performance at a couture boutique in her hometown of Leipzig. Two years later, in 1830, she gave her first full concert. As the decade progressed, Wieck traveled with Clara around Europe, building up her talent and her reputation. She played in Paris—the place to make it as a pianist at the time—and met the likes of Felix Mendelssohn and Frédéric Chopin. Soon she was on an equal footing with her male contemporaries and considered the "European Queen of Piano." In 1838, when she was just nineteen, she was honored by the Austrian court and received coveted membership to Vienna's Society of the Friends of Music. Later in life she would become a prolific composer and a respected piano teacher in her own right.

Courting Love

She'd achieved everything her father had hoped for and more, but in one fundamental way, she displeased him. As a teenager, Clara fell in love with Robert Schumann, a fellow composer and pianist who had studied under Wieck and lived in the family home. At the time, Schumann was yet to realize his great success, and his penniless status made him an unsatisfactory match, in Wieck's eyes. When he found out about their blossoming relationship, he forbade that the two see each other, threatening Clara's career and even Schumann's life. After some time apart, their minds were still set, and when Clara turned eighteen, Schumann asked Wieck for his daughter's hand in marriage. Wieck refused, and a tumultuous three years followed. It ended in 1840 when the couple went to court to fight for their right to marry without Wieck's permission. The court consented, and the couple were free to wed. Their marriage resulted in eight children and ended with Schumann's death in 1856, after a protracted illness and confinement in a mental hospital.

An Affair to Remember

Though she had to sacrifice her own career for her husband's, Clara's compositions and performance skills were highly regarded. She was one of only a few musicians at the time to perform music from memory—it was considered arrogant at the time, but Clara was a trendsetter and more and more teachers encouraged students to memorize musical scores as the nineteenth century progressed. She also socialized with the great and the good of Europe's legendary classical music scene—she counted Pauline Viardot, Jenny Lind, Joseph Joachim, and Johannes Brahms as her friends. She was even rumored to have embarked on a relationship with the latter, who was Schumann's protégé, in the wake of her husband's death.

How did a novice nun revolutionize the circus?

Quebec-born Antoinette Comeau was a novice nun when she ran away to join the circus in 1928. In trapeze training she met her future husband, and the gravity-defying act "the Flying Concellos" was born.

Trapeze Team

Antoinette caught the circus bug when she was visiting her trapeze artist sister, Mickey. Antoinette's first aerial act involved her hanging from a leather strap by only her teeth—it was known as "Iron Jaw." When Mickey traveled to Bloomington, Illinois, to train during the winter, Antoinette went along, too. And it was at Eddie Ward's "The Flying Wards" training camp that she met Arthur Concello and fell in love. Antoinette never went back to the convent. When Eddie died, Arthur took over the camp and the two started training together. Before long they had formed their own act, "the Flying Concellos." By 1932, they were members of Ringling Bros. and Barnum and Bailey's "The Greatest Show on Earth." It was the world's largest traveling circus, and they toured as far as London, Berlin, and the famed Cirque d'Hiver in Paris.

Triple Threat

The daring triple somersault was popularized by Mexican trapeze artist Alfredo Codona, and when Codona retired in 1933, it was Arthur Concello who took the baton and flew with it. In 1937, at Madison Square Garden, Arthur and Antoinette made history when they both performed the triple in an aerial performance that stunned audiences. Antoinette was one of the first women to perform this daring feat, and she became known as the "greatest woman flier of all time."

Retiring from the Ring

In 1952, movie mogul Cecil B. DeMille decided to bring the circus to the big screen in *The Greatest Show on Earth*, a love triangle set in the big top starring Charlton Heston, Betty Hutton, and Cornel Wilde. The real circus troupe appeared in the film, including the Flying Concellos, and it was Antoinette's job to train Hutton for her starring role. Sadly, despite several shoulder surgeries to try and repair the wear and tear caused by her work, Antoinette had to hang up her leotard in 1953. And the Concellos' relationship didn't fare much better: they divorced in 1956. The marriage was over and so,

THREE TIMES A CHARM

The triple somersault was once considered a legendary feat in aerial acrobatics. Italian trapeze artists referred to it as *solto mortale* (the deadly leap) because the stunt was so dangerous. The speed required to pull it off puts the brain in a spin that makes it harder for the flier to know when to reach out for the catcher. If they miss, they face dropping to the net, presuming one is in place, and potentially career-ending injuries. Among the first daredevils to complete the triple successfully was Russian gymnast Lena Jordan. She performed it in Australia in 1897, when she was just seventeen or eighteen (records differ) and later joined the Barnum & Bailey Circus, completing the stunt nearly thirty times.

it appeared, was Antoinette's career. But retirement wasn't on the cards just yet—John Ringling North asked her to become the circus's aerial director, a position she held for the next thirty years. In 1962 she was inducted into the Circus Hall of Fame.

Who were the first women to perform on the London stage?

Until 1660, female roles in theater were performed by men or teenage boys. Then King Charles II was restored to the throne and women graced London's stages for the first time.

A Royal Proclamation

While aristocratic women had been putting on plays in private from the early seventeenth century, public performances were a different matter. All theater was banned in 1647 under Cromwell's Puritanical Commonwealth of England. Then with Charles II's ascension, two theater companies were granted licenses. In 1662, the king decreed that "all the women's parts to be acted in either of the said two companies for the time to come may be portrayed by women." A few actresses had already tentatively tread the boards.

- In 1660, Thomas Killigrew's company had staged a production of Shakespeare's *Othello* at the Vere Street Theatre with a woman in the role of Desdemona. The play included a prologue that warned the crowd of what was to come.

- Historians believe the actress, whose presence no doubt shocked audiences, was Anne Marshall, also known as Mrs. Quin—both Marshall and her younger sister Rebecca were celebrities of the period. Other actresses to face this early scrutiny (and leering male theatergoers who paid extra to watch them dress in the wings) included Margaret Hughes, who joined the Theatre Royal company, Ann Street Barry, and Mary Saunderson, who was the first woman to play both Lady Macbeth and Juliet in *Romeo and Juliet*.

The King's Mistress

These first actresses came from a variety of backgrounds—but being able to read, remember lines, sing, and dance were prerequisites of the profession. One woman who rose through the ranks thanks to her theatrical prowess was Nell Gwyn. In a film-worthy rags-to-riches tale, she started off as the daughter of a pauper and a brothel owner, selling oranges to the audience at the Drury Lane Theatre, before catching the eye of Charles Hart, the theater's leading man. Despite being illiterate, she made her own first appearance in 1665. For the next few years she had audiences rolling in the aisles as part of the King's Company. This was how she came to the attention of Charles II. From 1669 she was one of the king's many mistresses (and the only one the public liked). She quit the theater for a life as a kept woman, having two sons by Charles—one of which became the Duke of St. Albans.

LOOSE WOMEN

They might have been the celebrities of their day, but by the mid-eighteenth century it was still hard for actresses to shake the association with scandal and prostitution. It didn't help that the main theaters were based in Covent Garden, where a number of brothels were also located. A few men continued to play female characters, despite the rise in real actresses. But they weren't the only cross-dressers cavorting on the stage. Women like Dorothea Jordan and Peg Woffington took on "breeches" roles where they performed as men. While these comedy performances were widely praised, they led to wider debates about female decorum.

What did Anna Pavlova ask for on her deathbed?

In 1931, just shy of her fiftieth birthday, Russian ballet legend Anna Pavlova succumbed to pneumonia while touring in The Hague. She had refused treatment that might have saved her when she learned it would mean the end of her dancing career.

A Dancer to the End

"If I can't dance, then I'd rather be dead," Pavlova reportedly told her doctors. According to her obituary in the *New York Times*, the doctors performed an operation to withdraw water from one of her lungs and administered a "Pasteur vaccine," but it was too late. Her husband and accompanist, Victor d'Andre, was by her bedside when she died at the Hotel des Indes, but it is believed that it was to her dresser that she uttered her infamous last words: "Get my swan costume ready."

A Life on Pointe

Outside of ballet circles, Pavlova's name today probably has more association with the meringue dessert than the dancer herself (it was named after her, by the way). But she is considered one of the most influential ballerinas of the twentieth century and was the first ballerina to tour around the world, clocking over 350,000 miles and wowing audiences with her talent.

"If I can't dance, then I'd rather be dead . . ."

Her start in ballet came after her mother took her to see *The Sleeping Beauty* at St. Petersburg's Imperial Mariinsky Theater. She would make her own official debut there some years later in *Les Dryades prétendues* ("The False Dryads"). But her rise to the top wouldn't be easy. With thin ankles, long limbs, and arched feet, she didn't fit the mold and was initially rejected from the Imperial Ballet School. When she finally did make the cut, she had to prove herself, taking extra classes and studiously improving her form.

Leaping to Great Heights

Even with all the extra hours, when Pavlova graduated, it was the audience who helped propel her to great heights, rather than her dance skills. She flouted the strict teachings of ballet master and principal choreographer Marius Petipa, but her energy and enthusiasm for ballet was infectious—her legions of fans called themselves Pavlovatzi, and she soon won Petipa over, too. She took on some of the greatest roles of the era, including the titular *Paquita* and *Giselle*, and in 1906, when she was twenty-five, she was named prima ballerina (the second highest rank for a female dancer).

THE DYING SWAN

The role that Pavlova was most renowned for was *The Dying Swan*. The solo dance was choreographed by Mikhail Fokine specifically for her. Set to Camille Saint-Saëns' *Le Cygne* from *Le Carnaval des animaux*, it was first staged in 1905. Pavlova is believed to have performed the four-minute ballet around 4,000 times during her life. After a successful American tour in 1910, she was summoned to the royal box of Czar Nicolas II of Russia where he congratulated her and said: "I so much regret that despite all I hear about your wonderful swan dance, I have never seen it." When she settled in London in 1912, she kept swans in an ornamental lake in her garden to study their movements.

Who was the first female film director?

In 1895, when Auguste and Louis Lumière held their first demonstration of projected film in Paris, secretary Alice Guy-Blaché was in the audience. She would become one of the first people to use film to tell a story.

Shooting a Story

Guy-Blaché worked at Léon Gaumont's photography company and asked him for permission to use the cameras. But unlike other documentary-style footage being shot at the time, of moving trains or crowds of people, Guy-Blaché wanted to use the equipment to tell a story. Her first narrative film, *The Cabbage Fairy*, featured a woman dressed as a fairy discovering babies in a cabbage patch. Soon she was head of Gaumont's film studio and experimenting with special effects and exposure techniques. Her most successful movie for Gaumont was 1906's *The Life of Christ*. The extravagant 30-minute-long film included over 300 extras and twenty-five sets.

Motion-Picture Maverick

In 1907 she married cameraman Herbert Blaché. The couple moved to the United States and eventually set up their own production house in Queens, New York called Solax, and built a state-of-the-art film studio. Between 1896 and 1920, Guy-Blaché wrote, directed, or produced around 600 silent films and 150 synchronized sound films—at one point she was directing three a week. In an industry dominated by men, her films stood out for their heroic female characters, gender-swapping antics, and emphasis on equality in marriage. She left the United States and filmmaking in 1922, after the couple divorced, returning to her native France with their children. She lectured and wrote widely on the industry, but never shot another film again.

SHOW BUSINESS

It's true what they say, there's no business like show business, which is why you should have no problem getting down to business and answering these questions. Lights, camera, ACTION!

Questions

1. What did Edith Piaf insist upon when she was asked to sing for German soldiers?

2. Where were the two Yoko Ono and John Lennon "Bed-ins" held?

3. Which dancer was *The Dying Swan* ballet created for?

4. What was Joanna Baillie's famous collection of plays called?

5. What was the Motion Picture Production Code more commonly known as?

6. What did Antoinette Concello do before she joined the circus?

7. Who did Marilyn Monroe famously sing "Happy Birthday" to in 1962?

8. Who directed the 1906 film *The Life of Christ*?

9. What was unusual about the Vere Street Theatre 1660 production of *Othello*?

10. Which famous composer was Clara Schumann rumored to have had a relationship with after her husband's death?

Turn to page 217 for the answers.

WHAT PHILOSOPHICAL SCHOOL DID HYPATIA BELONG TO?

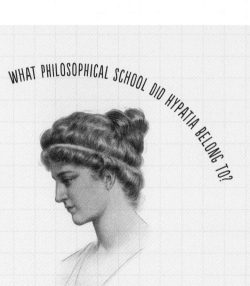

WHAT WAS ELIZABETH MAGIE'S BOARD GAME CALLED?

IN THE MOSUO CULTURE, WHAT ARE AXIA?

WHAT DID MARGARET THATCHER STUDY AT OXFORD UNIVERSITY?

GEORGIANA CAVENDISH WAS ACCUSED OF OFFERING WHAT TO "AN IMPRACTICABLE BUTCHER"?

QUIZ ANSWERS

WHAT IS THE CHEMICAL ELEMENT POLONIUM NAMED AFTER?

WHAT DID EGYPTIAN PHARAOHS WEAR TO ASSOCIATE THEMSELVES WITH THE GOD OSIRIS?

QUIZ ANSWERS

Politics Quiz Answers
1. Democratically elected female president.
2. Chemistry.
3. The Women's Christian Temperance Union.
4. Marat's assassin, Charlotte Corday.
5. Buenos Aires.
6. Pay social visits to Peggy Eaton.
7. Kisses in exchange for votes.
8. Rafael Trujillo.
9. The League of German Girls.
10. *Vanar Sena* ("the Monkey Brigade").

Feminism Quiz Answers
1. Manitoba Premier Sir Rodmond Roblin.
2. 1893.
3. Tennis player Bobby Riggs beat female ranked number one Margaret Court.
4. Savitribai Phule.
5. Ohio.
6. New York Radical Women.
7. Anmer.
8. A reference book or passbook.
9. Simone de Beauvoir.
10. Norman Rockwell.

Pioneers Quiz Answers

1. To make money for her round-the-world cycling trip.
2. *Chaika*, or Seagull.
3. Maria Telkes.
4. Weave straw with silk and thread to make hats.
5. Ada Lovelace.
6. Sell outfits as separates.
7. A "Secret Communication System."
8. *The Landlord's Game*.
9. Elizabeth Bisland.
10. A car cover.

Thinkers Quiz Answers

1. 1955.
2. Duchess of Newcastle, Margaret Cavendish.
3. Lise Meitner.
4. Marie Curie's home country of Poland.
5. Become a Benedictine nun.
6. The Penny Black.
7. The Neoplatonic school of philosophy.
8. Because her lab's director considered it. bad luck to bring women along.
9. Annie Jump Cannon.
10. Albert Einstein.

Leaders Quiz Answers

1. She cannot be elected president because she has foreign-born children.
2. A cane.
3. Thirty-four years.
4. A false metallic beard.
5. Catherine the Great.
6. A pearl earring in vinegar.
7. Political propaganda pamphlets.
8. A son.
9. The Golden Stool.
10. Ceruse.

Religion and Culture Quiz Answers

1. Sisters of Loreto.
2. For endorsing the practice of *kumbh vivaha* or "pot marriage."
3. Twelve.
4. Catholicism.
5. As a young man, he'd trained to be a Catholic priest.
6. Male lovers.
7. An unqualified doctor rubbed mustard paste in her eyes when she was a child.
8. Ann Lee.
9. The Second Great Awakening.
10. I love you.

Warriors and Superwomen Quiz Answers

1. Murderer's Row.
2. Camulodunum (Colchester).
3. Special Operations Executive.
4. She was the first Soviet citizen to be welcomed there.
5. Sally Ride (in 1983).
6. A cat.
7. One hundred.
8. The Hudson and the Harlem.
9. The Muscogee Creeks.
10. A kaiken.

Crime and Punishment Quiz Answers

1. Baltimore.
2. Scandinavia.
3. Ergot fungus found in rye or wheat.
4. Georgia Ann Robinson.
5. A levered seat contraption used to submerge women in the river for their crimes.
6. The practice whereby poor women, usually single mothers, would pay a "baby farmer" to take their child off their hands.
7. Buffalo Bill's.
8. Police station matron.
9. Serfs.
10. An ax.

Arts and Literature Quiz Answers

1. To see if she was telling the truth about what had happened.
2. DDT.
3. She heard a request on the radio from the exiled Dutch government for eyewitness accounts of people suffering under occupation and wanted to prepare her diary for publication.
4. 1910—the year the Mexican Revolution began.
5. It showed Cleopatra deceased.
6. *The Tale of Genji*.
7. Weaving.
8. Tom.
9. 1,550 miles.
10. A Pulitzer Prize.

Show Business Quiz Answers

1. That French POWs could watch her perform, too.
2. Amsterdam and Montreal.
3. Anna Pavlova.
4. *Plays on the Passions*.
5. The Hays Code.
6. She was a novice nun.
7. President John F. Kennedy.
8. Alice Guy-Blaché.
9. It featured a woman in the role of Desdemona—the first time a woman had been on the London stage.
10. Johannes Brahms.

INDEX

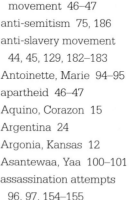

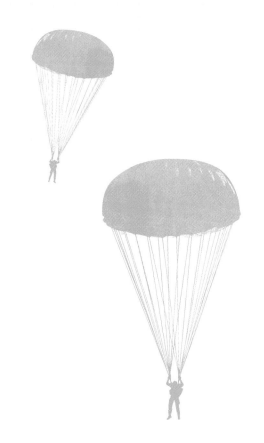

CREDITS